# By a Thread

*and*

# The Raft

**Lucy Gough** has written extensively for radio and stage and since 1996 has been a scriptwriter for *Hollyoaks*. Her work includes *Catherine Wheel* (1991, toured by Scallywag Theatre-in-Education Company); *Our Lady Of Shadows* (1994, BBC Radio 3); *As To Be Naked (Is the Best Disguise)* (1994, Theatr Clwyd Theatre-in-Education), *Crossing The Bar* (toured 1994), shortlisted BBC Wales Writer of the Year Award 1994 and John Whiting Award 1994; *Rushes* (1995, Arad Coch); *Head* (1996, BBC Radio 4); *Wolfskin* (1997); *Prophetess of Exeter* (1997, BBC World Service); *The Red Room* (1999, BBC Radio 4); *The Mermaid's Tail* (1999, BBC Radio 4); *Judith Beheading Holofernes* (2000, BBC Radio 4); *Mapping The Soul* (2001, Aberystwyth Arts Centre); *Gryfhead* (2003, Welsh tour and Dublin); *Wuthering Heights* (2003, *Woman's Hour* series, BBC Radio 4); and *Mapping the Soul* (2005, BBC Radio 4). She is a lecturer in radio drama at the University of Wales Aberystwyth, and Lampeter.

Lucy Gough

# By a Thread
*and*
# The Raft

Published by Methuen 2006

Methuen Publishing Limited
11–12 Buckingham Gate
London SW1E 6LB

10 9 8 7 6 5 4 3 2 1

Copyright © Lucy Gough 2006

Lucy Gough has asserted her rights under
the Copyright, Designs and Patents Act, 1988,
to be identified as the author of this work

Methuen Publishing Limited Reg. No. 3543167

A CIP catalogue record for this book is available from
the British Library

ISBN 0 413 77581 X

Typeset by Country Setting, Kingsdown, Kent
Printed and bound in Great Britain by
Bookmarque Ltd, Croydon, Surrey

**Caution**

# Introduction

I was commissioned by Theatr Iolo to write *By a Thread*. The initial brief (which was deliberately broad), given by the director Kevin Lewis, was to write a play about all the changes taking place in the world, a brief I found both inspiring and daunting..

At the time I was writing this play Yugoslavia was breaking up and so war became central to our discussions. It seemed to me, however, that there was room to explore the issues of war alongside a more personal, individual experience of change that takes place during adolescence, a time in our lives when there is an edge and an attitude to life which is never quite the same again. All those things which we meet in life are visited for the first time and new boundaries are tested: life, death, sex, all of the 'stuff of life' which we spend the rest of our lives dealing with often has its first impact then. The innocence of those first meetings; the rawness, the pain and the joy creates an energy which as a writer I find inspiring. The courage and the fear of this time in our lives is something that as we get older we tend unfortunately to forget. All this testing of boundaries, experimentation with life, is done with an attitude, a cockiness, a sense of immortality that doesn't last. There's an arrogance towards life which passes, after which we often cling to life with grim determination. People are discovering their own emotional baggage, their boundaries, and it's all so new for each person, new and different.

Therefore it felt appropriate to explore the huge questions and issues that war raises while also using it as a metaphor for that interior shift from child to adult – that sense of unease, unpredictability, even danger, where the boundaries are shifting and it's hard to know where the old ones end and the new ones start.

War and adolescence are both heightened experiences, and my feeling was that the backdrop of a young couple travelling up a mountain to escape war, and being thrown together in such extreme circumstances, gave plenty of room to explore some of the big questions about being alive, about being human. To this end I created four characters, all of whom are struggling with huge changes in their lives, all of whom either won't or can't let go of things, or in the case of the Old Lady want to let go of everything.

At heart, *By a Thread* is a love story, but within this such issues as survival, jealousy, death, responsibility and the necessity to create our own structures are explored while also discussing the grim reality of war.

The idea for *The Raft*, the second play in this volume, was triggered when I heard a documentary programme about a prison for young teenage women where the suicide rate is very high. Most of the women were single mothers and addicted to drugs . . . and until recently their job in prison was to sew shrouds. I couldn't quite believe the short-sightedness of this: young women already separated from their children – the only thing in their lives likely to offer hope – and they were employed to sew shrouds, thereby reinforcing the absence of hope except in death. And this at the end of the twentieth century!

What happened to empathy, to rehabilitation, to anything that goes deeper than punishing those who for the most part are vulnerable young people adrift, abandoned by society? So I wrote a play about it, knowing it wouldn't change the situation but there wasn't much else I could do.

I contacted Peter Leslie Wild, a radio producer I had enjoyed working with on several other projects and who I knew would 'get' what I was trying to do with this play. He submitted the idea for commission and it was accepted.

Different plays get written in different ways. This one came as a whole. I knew immediately the story, the pace, the tone; I could hear the rhythm, I could almost beat out every footstep of the gaoler, the girl's journey to the bottom of the sea, and her heartbeat as she wrestles her life back.

I had heard a singer (Jeff Buckley) whose delicate vulnerable voice seemed to encapsulate the mood, the sense of frailty in this play, so I played his album all the time I was writing it, to infuse the atmosphere of the play. I also used the music in the play as another layer of meaning and atmosphere.

I knew that central to the play was an image drawn from the famous painting by Gericault called *The Raft of the Medusa*. It had always struck me as a potent image of those disposed of by society, those cut adrift, abandoned, driven to devour each other to survive. It was an image I had been carrying around for a long time waiting for the right play.

In the play there is therefore a creaking raft with a 'chorus of shrouds' who act as sails, as well as hunters, as they circumnavigate the dark edges of the mind like sharks hunting down the vulnerable to pull them onto this raft of despair.

The fact that such a way of telling a story is possible is the joy of writing for radio. This ability to cut straight to a metaphorical landscape is one that I have always felt tells the real truth of our lives, searches out the underbelly and tells it how it is.

In radio drama the relationship between the audience and the play is direct and intimate, which means that hopefully the audience will for forty-five minutes inhabit the mind of the central character, Maggie; they will understand and feel her despair as she journeys to the bottom of the sea and then, having felt the depth of her despair, they will feel the tiny impulse for life that flickers there and her courage and strength as she wrestles back to life.

Sometimes when we empathise for a little while with someone outside our usual frame of reference, we understand something new and maybe this does change things a little . . .

Lucy Gough

# By a Thread

*By a Thread* was commissioned and produced by Theatr Iolo. It was first performed at Cathays High School, Cardiff, on 17 September 1992. The cast was as follows:

| | |
|---|---|
| **Boy** | Alistair Leith |
| **Girl** | Mai Lu |
| **Old Lady** | Martine Palmer |
| **Soldier** | Paul Cowan |

| | |
|---|---|
| *Director* | Kevin Lewis |
| *Designer* | Kim Kenny |
| *Music* | Tim Farrell |
| *Assistant Director* | Nia Davies |

## Characters

**Boy**
**Girl**
**Old Lady**
**Soldier**

*On a mountainside.*

*A wall and in another area a bed with a moth-eaten patchwork quilt over it, in the rubble of a building. There is also a hidden trench. Behind the wall there are sounds of giggling etc., an occasional limb appears. This can be taken as far as is appropriate. A young couple emerge rearranging their clothing, the* **Girl** *is annoyed, the* **Boy** *confused.*

**Boy**
> Why?

*The* **Girl** *is looking out.*

> It's safe . . .

**Girl**
> Not that.

**Boy**
> I don't understand.

**Girl**
> I'm cold.

*Exasperated, the* **Boy** *goes to his rucksack and takes out a knife, finds a bit of wood and starts hacking at it.*

**Boy**
> I could warm you up.

**Girl**
> Nothing looks real.

**Boy**
> What's real?

**Girl**
> Don't.

**Boy**
> Well?

**Girl**
> What you saying?

**Boy**
> Down there isn't real. We're real, you and me together
> we're real. I can see you, feel you, talk to you, love you, that
> makes you real to me and me feel real, see?

**Girl**
> No.

**Boy** (*cuts himself with knife*)
> Ouch!

*The* **Girl** *goes over to look.*

**Girl**
> I'm scared.

**Boy**
> There's a lot to be scared of.

**Girl**
> I mean, us.

**Boy**
> You're scared of that?

**Girl**
> It's still important.

**Boy**
> We're not talking murder here . . .

**Girl**
> I have to decide.

**Boy**
> I need you.

*The* **Girl** *goes to the edge of the mountain and puts her arms out.*

**Girl**
> I'm standing on the edge of the world.

**Boy**
> Jump.

**Girl**
> I might hurt.

**Boy**
>  You might fly.

**Girl**
>  You trying to get rid of me?

*The* **Boy** *goes over to her.*

**Boy**
>  Be brave about us.

*He starts to spin her round and round.*

**Girl**
>  Uuh! I feel sick. Stop! I can't . . .

**Boy**
>  I don't know who's going faster, me or the world.

*They go faster and faster, finally falling onto the ground, dizzy. Both look up at the sky.*

**Girl**
>  The faster you go, the slower time goes.

*She sits up and looks out, then the* **Boy** *does as well.*

>  Up here we can see everything, the whole world, but differently.

**Boy**
>  Like when you squint your eyes up . . .

**Girl**
>  Kaleidoscopic, giddy, dizzy, shifting, fragmented.

**Boy**
>  If I didn't like my dinner I'd squint my eyes so it all blurred together, then I could eat it.

**Girl**
>  There's a rainbow wrapping itself round a mountain, and over there apple blossom on a red rug after a picnic . . .

**Boy**
>  Stop it!

**Girl**
Why?

**Boy**
You're making pretty pictures out of misery.

**Girl**
It's a way of coping, I look out and change what I see. You look in and ignore it.

**Boy**
Looking at it, having it shoved down my throat, isn't going to change it, it's over, the world's over. Mad. Looking at it won't stop people suffering. At least my dinner was edible even if it didn't look it.

**Girl**
Can you shut it all out then, feel nothing?

**Boy**
I saw that rainbow you're talking about, I watched them. A mass of brightly dressed refugees struggling up a mountain. They were scared witless. They would die if they stayed and death sure as hell was waiting for them on the mountain. I just watched. I felt nothing. I could smell their fear, but my heart felt hard. Then I saw a small boy trying to keep up – he had a T-shirt on with a picture of a lion on the front, and I felt it all. But it's too much, we must keep it out.

**Girl**
I can't shut out the picture of my house, their faces.

**Boy** (*holds her*)
We're safe here.

**Girl**
How can we be safe anywhere? You saw what's happening, nothing sacred, nothing safe, nothing, nothing, nothing!

**Boy**
Listen. (*Shakes her.*) Listen, if you think like that we're finished. We've got each other. We can hold each other together. Keep something tight. This is nowhere, no time,

no place, so we can make it what we want. Up here away from it all, we can start again. Maybe all this has happened before.

**Girl**

What?

**Boy**

The world destroying itself. Us, we, you and me can start again. Paradise, get it right this time. Together.

**Girl**

Don't rush me.

**Boy**

There's no one to stop you now!

**Girl**

I have to think, I have laws, my laws. Let me think, don't push me.

**Boy**

Don't you love me?

**Girl**

That's not fair.

**Boy**

Well?

**Girl**

I just have to keep control of my own life, I've nothing, no family, nothing, everything is going to change, I have to know *me*.

**Boy**

Great! Alone on a mountain with a beautiful girl, nothing to stop us, and she wants to think.

**Girl**

I can't explain how I feel, it's hard, I wish I knew how to explain it better.

**Both**

Do you love me?

*They laugh.*

*The **Boy** hands her the carved wood.*

**Boy**
A token.

*The **Girl** places it against the wall. The **Boy** returns to his carving, but also sifts through the earth for flints to make arrowheads.*

*There is a loud explosion of rock music and a **Soldier** appears out of the trench. This is a total surprise for the audience.*

**Soldier**
It's bitter cold at night, since the fight.
Ssh! Boys, what's that noise?

*The **Soldier** dives onto his belly and lies still, very watchful, looking into the audience. The **Boy** is still carving.*

**Girl**
Now what you doing?

**Boy**
Arrows.

**Girl**
What?

**Boy**
I'm making arrows.

**Girl**
Why?

**Boy**
For food.

**Girl**
I don't believe this.

**Boy**
I'll spear a rabbit.

**Girl** (*sarcastically*)
Yes!

**Boy**

If I practice.

**Girl**

They don't keep still.

**Boy**

I'm making a bow as well.

**Girl**

We're not playing a game!

**Boy**

You think of something better.

**Girl**

We'll have to go into one of the towns.

**Boy**

It's deadly down there.

**Girl**

Collect berries and leaves, then. Some of them are bound to be all right to eat.

**Boy**

I need meat.

**Girl**

What happens to rabbits when they die of old age?

**Boy**

I can catch one, you'll see, then you'll have to skin it, that's the woman's job.

**Girl**

No.

**Boy**

Coward.

**Girl**

It'll make me sick, I'm a vegetarian.

**Boy**

Not if you're hungry enough. You'll eat anything if you're hungry enough, I might eat you.

*He makes a dive for her, playfully bites her and steals her school tie.*

**Girl** (*she attempts to push him away*)
    Go catch a rabbit.

**Boy** (*still holding her*)
    This decision-making is for a different world.

*The **Girl** tries to grab the tie; he keeps it.*

**Boy**
    I need . . .

**Girl** (*gives him a hard shove*)
    That'd better be a joke.

*The **Boy** returns to his arrows, muttering, and starts bending a stick to make a bow. During the following dialogue he is making a bow with the tie and stick. The **Girl** takes a notebook and pencil out of her bag; she lies down on her stomach and, using her arm to hide what she is doing, proceeds to write. The **Boy** is very curious.*

**Girl**
    How long do you think we'll be here?

**Boy**
    I don't know.

**Girl**
    Years?

**Boy**
    Could be. What you doing?

**Girl**
    Writing. What are we going to do with ourselves?

**Boy**
    Survive. Writing what?

**Girl**
    My diary. Will we grow up, or will being here mean we just stay like this?

**Boy**
    Of course we'll grow up. Why you writing in a diary?

**Girl**

Somewhere to put how I feel. It's not stupid. Time's just a theory, there's no such thing as absolute time, it's all relative to where you are and who you're with, something like that. So being up here with just you could mean . . .

**Boy**

. . . time is just a way of measuring change.

**Girl**

Yes, but maybe it's different now.

**Boy**

You're the scientist.

**Girl**

I wanted to be.

**Boy** (*in a* Star Trek *voice*)

This is captain's log, star date . . .

**Girl**

Stop it!

**Boy**

You can see how things change with your diary, keep a record and look back at it. Can I read it?

**Girl**

Diaries are secret. There's none of the things here which make you grow up at home.

**Boy**

We'll grow up together.

**Girl**

What happened to choice?

**Boy**

At least we're alive. We shouldn't have secrets, you and me.

**Girl**

I need to think alone.

**Boy**

Will you write about me?

**Girl**

I'll write about everything. I do love you. I didn't mean . . . about choice.

**Boy**

I know. But you need secrets?

**Girl**

I need space. It's not like it was. No Mum to tell me off, I have to tell myself off. Watch over myself. I'll watch over you. We should make some rules.

**Boy**

Like making the age of consent seventy-five?

**Girl**

Oh, stop it! Surely the whole basis of this new order isn't going to be sex.

**Boy**

We don't need rules.

**Girl**

Who's in charge of wood?

**Boy**

You.

**Girl**

Who tidies the shelter?

**Boy**

You.

**Girl**

Who cooks?

**Boy**

You.

**Girl**

See, that's why we need rules.

**Boy**

I'm the hunter.

*He gathers up his bow and arrows as if off to hunt.*

**Girl**
   I can see that, Big Chief Running Rabbit.

**Boy**
   You'll see – I saw some planes dropping parcels, a few
   landed on a ridge further down, I'll see if I can reach them.

*He starts to go. She grabs his arm.*

**Girl**
   Be careful.

*They kiss.*

**Boy**
   I won't be long.

**Girl**
   Keep your head down.

*They kiss.*

**Boy**
   I'll be all right.

**Girl**
   I'm nothing without you.

*They kiss again.*

**Boy**
   On the other hand –

*He moves towards her again, she moves away, he leaves.*

   Keep the bed warm for me.

**Girl**
   Hush.

**Boy**
   Don't eat any apples while I'm gone.

*The **Girl** goes back to her diary and settles down to write.*

**Girl** (*to audience*)
I want to find the edge.
To know where I end and the world starts.
But the outline keeps changing.
He doesn't see that first I have to find my shape in the world.
Find out what pattern I make, where I fit,
before I can blur the edge with someone else.
It's bad enough the world keeps shifting, unsteady,
changing its outline.
I'm trying to fit into something which is as uncertain as me.

*The* **Boy** *comes in pulling a parcel: supplies wrapped up in a blanket with a parachute on the end.*

**Girl**
The hunter home from the hills.

**Boy**
Big buffalo dropped from sky.

**Girl**
I bet that took some killing.

**Boy**
Nearly killed me, it landed right on the edge of a ledge.

*The young couple open the parcel, find chocolate, start playfully to fight over it and then feed each other with it. They then wrap themselves up together in the parachute.*

**Girl**
Bound together for ever.

**Boy**
Siamese twins.

*They lie on their stomachs looking down below them.*

**Girl**
What is that line? It wasn't there yesterday.

**Boy**
A tribe.

**Girl**

But they're not moving.

**Boy**

Dead, they're all dead.

**Girl**

Why?

**Boy**

Why any of it?

**Girl**

All that water, those people drowning, and over there people dying of thirst. If I had a giant ladle . . .

**Boy**

You could dig a channel with your finger, like at the seaside and let the water flow.

**Girl**

Giant Finger saves the world.

**Boy**

Super Finger.

**Girl**

And I would put out all the oil fires, snuff them out like a candle.

**Boy**

Flick each of the bomber planes over on their backs.

**Girl**

We could play tiddlywinks with them.

**Boy**

Scoop up fields of rice and drop them where they're needed.

**Girl**

I wish we could. Oh, I wish we could.

**Boy**

What we've got here is all we can do.

**Girl**

It seems wrong.

**Boy**

We must survive, and that means leaving them to it.

**Girl**

I miss my friends. I've nobody to talk to.

**Boy**

Me.

**Girl**

That's not the same.

**Boy**

Why not.

**Girl**

It just isn't, it's different, you don't understand.

**Boy**

That's what the whole world says about the rest . . . that's the problem.

**Girl**

I'm sorry.

**Boy** (*starts to kiss her*)

If you're that sorry –

**Girl**

That's not fair.

**Boy**

It's getting dark. We'd best build a shelter.

*The* **Girl** *sorts out the rest of the food in the parcel and puts it in a hole in the wall.*

**Girl**

This won't last us long.

**Boy**

We'll be all right.

*He pulls in two canes, cuts them down a bit and makes tent poles out of them, starting to make a shelter. As he builds the shelter, the* **Girl** *does her best to make a bed. It is clearly an important task for her. The* **Boy** *grabs her round the waist. She tries to push him away.*

**Girl**

For now we just sleep together to keep warm.

*The* **Girl** *shakes out the blanket violently. As she does this, the* **Old Lady** *falls out of her bed. As the* **Old Lady** *talks, the couple get into bed. As the* **Old Lady** *picks herself up and dusts herself off, she shouts and shakes her fist.*

**Old Lady**

Missed . . . You missed again you great lumox. Young men behind tons of metal and you can't even hit an old lady lying on her bed waiting to die.

*She points to her stomach.*

Shall I paint a target on me belly? Could you hit me then?

*Still cursing, she starts to pull something out from under her bed − a sewing basket.*

Silly beggars!

*Starts to sew her quilt.*

The lot of them . . . worse than moths.

*As she pulls out a piece of metal from the quilt, the* **Boy** *and* **Girl** *are trying to get comfy in bed.*

**Girl**

I wish I had a mirror . . .

*The* **Boy** *grunts.*

**Girl**

I don't know who I am.

**Boy**

What did people do before mirrors, then?

**Girl**

How should I know?

**Boy**
I'll draw a picture of you.

**Girl**
That's how you see me, not how I see me.

**Boy**
So?

**Girl** (*suddenly scared, grabs the* **Boy***'s arm*)
That mountain, it's breathing

**Boy**
Don't be daft, it's all the people.

**Girl** (*insistent*)
But look, you can see it heaving up and down.

**Boy**
Because there's so many, they completely cover the mountain.

**Old Lady**
Flesh of the world.

**Girl**
It's all such a mess.

**Boy**
Chaos.

**Old Lady**
Falling apart at the seams.

**Girl**
Everywhere you look . . .

**Boy**
. . . death.

**Old Lady**
Coming undone.

**Girl**
What can we do?

**Boy**
We've got each other.

**Old Lady**
  Together, together, pull everything together.

**Girl**
  Hold me.

**Boy**
  Safe.

**Old Lady**
  Mend and heal.

**Boy**
  For ever?

**Girl**
  I don't know.

**Boy**
  Will you be mine for ever?

**Girl**
  Will we be here for ever?

*The* **Old Lady** *starts singing as the* **Boy** *and* **Girl** *go to sleep. The* **Soldier** *appears out of a trench; he crawls on his belly until he eventually comes across the* **Old Lady**.

**Old Lady**
  What are you doing?

**Soldier**
  What you doing?

**Old Lady**
  What do you mean, what am I doing ?

**Soldier**
  That noise.

**Old Lady**
  Singing.

**Soldier**
  We don't call that singing where I come from.

**Old Lady**
Singing.

**Soldier**
Why you sewing?

**Old Lady**
Mending.

**Soldier**
What's the point?

**Old Lady**
There's a lot of point . . . You staying there all day?

**Soldier**
This 'ere is combat position . . . best line of defence . . . be unseen.

**Old Lady**
Who's not supposed to see you? I can see you.

**Soldier**
Enemy.

**Old Lady**
Am I enemy?

**Soldier** (*gets up, but is very jumpy, holding his gun*)
You best move on.

**Old Lady**
I am not moving.

**Soldier**
You best.

**Old Lady**
This is my home.

**Soldier**
I'm telling you.

**Old Lady**
So?

**Soldier**
It's an order.

**Old Lady**
You're just a boy.

**Soldier**
A soldier.

**Old Lady**
Same thing.

**Soldier**
I could shoot you.

**Old Lady**
I'm terrified.

**Soldier**
Could.

*He points his gun at the* **Old Lady**, *very uncertainly, shaking.*

**Old Lady**
Go on then.

**Soldier** (*unconvincingly*)
I mean it.

**Old Lady**
How many you killed, Sonny?

**Soldier**
Don't call me Sonny.

**Old Lady**
How many?

**Soldier**
Stop asking me questions.

**Old Lady**
Go home, Sonny.

**Soldier**
I said don't call me Sonny.

**Old Lady**
What if I want to die . . . ?

**Soldier**
What you mean?

**Old Lady** (*pushes butt of gun*)
Put it away.

**Soldier** (*thrusts it back, trying to look aggressive*)
Don't push me.

*The* **Old Lady** *gets up.*

**Soldier**
Don't move.

**Old Lady**
You told me to move on.

**Soldier** (*confused*)
Get lost.

*The* **Old Lady** *starts to move off slowly, but suddenly turns – she has forgotten her quilt. Her sudden movement startles the* **Soldier** *who panics and fires, shooting her in the leg. The* **Soldier** *is horrified at what he has done and is unable to speak for a while.*

**Old Lady**
Ouch . . . you shot me . . . ouch . . .

**Soldier**
It was an accident, shh, don't scream.

**Old Lady**
I'm not screaming . . .

**Soldier**
You're not dead.

**Old Lady**
I can see that . . . If you want to kill someone, shoot them here –

*She points to her heart. Shouting.*

Useless . . . You're all the same. The whole world at war, one eighty-six-year-old lady wants to die and nobody can do it. I'm not staying here – at the rate you go, it'd be quicker to die of old age.

**Soldier**
Shh, they'll hear us.

**Old Lady**
Who'll hear us?

**Soldier**
The enemy.

**Old Lady**
You're the enemy – you shot me, I'm bleeding.

**Soldier**
You'll be all right, shh . . . I never meant to . . . I never shot anyone . . .

**Old Lady**
I might bleed to death, I suppose.

**Soldier**
I can stop the bleeding.

*He moves towards her.*

**Old Lady**
Don't come near me, you great lumox . . . all the same . . .

*She starts packing up her bag and then limps away, muttering and hurling back the odd insult.*

Call yourself a soldier . . .

**Soldier** (*shirty*)
I could have, if I wanted to!

**Old Lady**
You, and whose army? . . . Useless.

*She wanders away. The **Soldier** starts to move back to his trench.*

**Soldier**
I shot a hag . . . I shot a hag . . .

*He repeats the same line, using his gun as a guitar, and starts a heavy metal routine with the gun before jumping into the trench.*

*The* **Old Lady** *arrives at the camp, with the quilt wrapped around her shoulders. The young couple are under a blanket, asleep. Together they make a huge indefinable lump which occasionally moves, snores and grunts. The* **Old Lady** *is not sure what she has come upon.*

**Old Lady**
Man or beast?

*The couple move in their sleep.*

Maybe a dragon.

*She starts to move away.*

Dragons don't build shelters.

*She moves around them as they toss and turn, jumping if there is a loud noise. Then a foot appears.*

A foot . . .

*She grabs it.*

. . . a human foot.

*The* **Boy** *looks out.*

**Boy** (*to audience*)
Like a rattlesnake she entered our lair.

**Old Lady** (*as she finds another pair of feet*)
How many of you? Room for another?

**Boy** (*starts interrogating her*)
How did you find us? Which way did you come?

**Girl** (*looking at the wound*)
Leave her, she's bleeding.

**Boy**
There could be others . . .

**Girl**
She's hurt . . .

**Boy**
Soldiers . . .

**Old Lady**
I'm bleeding to death.

**Girl**
We must stop it.

*She goes to tear a strip off the shelter roof.*

**Old Lady**
Leave it, I'm dying.

**Boy**
What you doing?

**Girl**
I need a bandage.

**Boy**
That's our shelter.

**Girl**
Don't be daft . . .

**Boy**
Use that.

*He points at the quilt.*

**Old Lady** (*holding quilt*)
No!

**Boy**
Full of fleas.

**Old Lady**
It's all I got.

**Girl**
I can't leave her to bleed to death.

**Boy**
She's old, anyway.

**Old Lady** (*shouts*)
Eighty-six years and three months . . . I'll decide when I die, not you.

**Girl** (*gives the* **Boy** *look*)
I'll take it off the back.

*She gets the cloth and wraps up the* **Old Lady**'s *leg.*

We should take the bullet out.

*The* **Boy** *offers his knife in a menacing fashion. The* **Old Lady** *growls.*

**Girl**
It will have to come out.

**Old Lady**
NO!

*The* **Girl** *continues to wrap the wound.*

**Old Lady**
. . . Got any food?

**Girl**
Yes.

**Boy** (*very quickly*)
No, we don't.

*The* **Girl** *moves to the food-hole but the* **Boy** *blocks her way.*

**Girl**
You can't let her starve.

**Boy**
Why not?

**Old Lady**
Take too long.

**Girl**
You just can't.

**Boy**
If she thinks we've got food we'll never get rid of her.

**Girl**
We can't throw her out, anyway . . . where will she go?

**Boy**
She'll die anyway with that bullet in her.

**Girl**
If you love me –

**Boy**
I can think of better ways to show I love you.

**Girl**
Love is about compassion.

**Boy**
It's about passion . . .

**Girl**
. . . and compassion.

*The* **Boy** *unwillingly goes to the food-hole and hands the* **Girl** *some chocolate and dry biscuits. She hands them to the* **Old Lady** *who wolfs them down.*

**Old Lady** (*to the* **Boy**)
You remind me of the boys who used to stick their bare bums over my wall.

**Girl**
You look like my nan.

**Old Lady**
Occupational hazard of old age, once you're old you look like everybody's nan.

**Girl**
You sound bitter?

**Old Lady**
Just limited.

**Boy**
This is our place.

**Girl** (*to the* **Boy**)
Stop being so rude.

*To the* **Old Lady**.

He don't mean it.

**Boy**
I do.

**Girl**
No he don't.

**Boy**
Do, I do. There's not enough food. And what about us . . .
together . . . if she's here . . . ?

*The* **Girl** *is not taking any notice. The* **Boy** *challenges her.*

**Boy**
. . . Kiss me.

**Girl** (*embarrassed*)
Not now.

**Boy**
When then?

**Girl**
Sshshshsh.

**Boy** (*to audience*)
It's going to be just like having her mum around . . . just
when I thought the collapse of the world had its good side.

*He picks up his knife and goes off in a sulk behind a rock; he is hacking
at a stick again. The* **Old Lady** *lays her quilt out and settles herself.*

**Boy** (*to audience, as he hacks at stick*)
I never explain it right . . . She reads me wrong and that
makes it come out worse. We have to be tough . . . What
can I do? Except keep her and me alive. I saw two kids
wrapped up in a blanket, I thought I'll save them. I went
to pick them up, they were cold, dead, their lives hardly
started . . . Justice has died here . . . There's new laws . . .

jungle laws . . . 'Extra' will pull us down, we have to be hard.

*The* **Old Lady** *takes out her sewing.*

**Girl**
Why you sewing?

**Old Lady** (*as she threads the needle and cotton*)
There's things you do . . . put the inside and the outside together.

**Girl**
I wish I could mend the world.

**Old Lady**
You'd have to break the skin.

**Girl** (*concentrating on sewing*)
It's hard keeping it neat.

**Old Lady**
What's easy?

**Girl**
Do you really want to die?

**Old Lady**
At eighty-six . . . ?

**Girl**
Aren't you scared?

**Old Lady**
I was scared when the war started.
Dodging death,
hanging onto life.
By a thread.
Then I thought it's hope that's killing me,
trying to stay alive.
So I decided I wanted to die.
I let go.
Eighty-six is a good age to live dangerously,
I've nothing to lose.

**Girl**
I don't like the danger – everything shifting, changing fast.

**Old Lady**
Freedom comes with age.

**Girl** (*still sewing and pulling the thread tight as she does so*)
I can see it all so clearly from up here . . . what needs to be done. I could make a pattern from the chaos.

**Old Lady**
The higher you go the clearer it gets.
The older you are the lighter your life.

*The* **Soldier** *stumbles into camp; he is again using his gun as a guitar and is miles away. He notices the camp; when he realises there are people he raises his gun. The* **Soldier** *moves slowly to tent and peers in. The* **Old Lady** *and he spot each other at the same time.*

**Old Lady**
You!

**Soldier**
The hag!

**Old Lady**
Come to finish me?

**Soldier**
I didn't mean . . . they taught me.

*The* **Boy** *has spotted the* **Soldier** *and is creeping up behind with his knife.*

**Old Lady**
What they teach you?

**Soldier**
To kill.

**Old Lady**
No good at learning, then.

**Soldier**
It was an accident.

**Old Lady**
    Trained killer.

**Soldier** (*to the* **Girl**)
    Can't you shut her up?

**Girl**
    What do you want?

**Soldier**
    Nothing . . . I . . .

*The* **Boy** *leaps on him and holds the knife to his throat.*

**Boy**
    Drop the gun!

*The* **Soldier** *drops it.*

**Old Lady**
    Cut him . . . cut him!

**Girl**
    Don't hurt him . . .

*To the* **Old Lady**.

    Did you mean that?

**Boy**
    Throw your bag over there.

**Soldier** (*takes off bag and throws it to the* **Old Lady** *and the* **Girl**)
    Check there's no weapons in it.

*The* **Soldier** *tries to say something. The* **Boy** *stops him. The* **Girl**
*opens the bag and screams.*

**Soldier**
    What is it? What's the matter?

**Girl**
    A head . . . there's a head in here!

*She drops the bag and runs to the* **Old Lady**, *who comforts her.*

**Soldier** (*manages to shout*)
    Mate . . . it's my mate.

**Old Lady**
What did he ask for, a haircut?

**Boy**
Bring it here.

*They bring it over tentatively; he looks in, retches and hands it to the* **Soldier**, *who holds it tight.*

**Soldier**
It's my mate. We came to fight together . . . I couldn't leave him . . . he's my mate.

**Boy**
It stinks.

**Soldier**
Don't say that about my mate.

**Boy**
What you going to do with it?

**Soldier**
We're going fishing.

**Boy**
You what?

**Soldier**
Before . . . We used to before . . . before all this.

**Boy** (*points to head*)
Plenty of bait.

*The* **Soldier** *makes the head in bag growl and go for the* **Boy**. *The* **Boy** *steps back, scared, and then tries to regain composure.*

**Boy**
Stop being so bloody daft!

**Soldier**
Weren't me.

**Boy**
Course it was!

**Soldier**
> Weren't.

**Boy**
> You're cracked.

**Soldier**
> The others were cracked . . . like plates . . . bits everywhere. The world hawked up its dead . . . everywhere . . . I didn't know which bits were my mate . . . I found his head.

**Boy**
> It's just a head.

**Soldier**
> We're going fishing. I'm looking for water that isn't full of blood and oil . . . I thought up here. I want to find somewhere clean and sit there with my mate . . . I want to forget.

**Boy** (*to the* **Girl**)
> We must move on, these two found us, it's all getting closer. We must head further up the mountain, away from the chaos.

**Girl**
> What about them?

**Boy**
> That's their problem, not ours . . . I've told you . . . we must survive . . . help each other . . . nobody else.

**Girl**
> I can't leave her . . . it'd be like leaving my nan.

**Boy**
> Don't be daft.

**Girl**
> I'm not.

**Old Lady**
> I can't walk far, my leg throbs like an army of tanks.

**Girl**
> I won't leave you.

**Old Lady**
Reckon this is it.

**Soldier**
It's my fault you're hurt.

*The **Boy** has started to take down the tent.*

**Boy**
None of you are coming with us. Me and my girl had a nice time till you bust in . . . you have no right to come between us.

**Soldier**
Safety in numbers.

**Boy**
An old lady and a soldier who can't shoot straight . . . I don't think we're missing much. Things were just beginning to work out for us.

**Girl**
I'm not going anywhere unless they do. We can't leave them.

**Boy**
How are we going to get anywhere if she can't walk?

**Soldier** (*starts to pull at tent*)
Here, look.

*He starts to build a stretcher with two canes and the blanket.*

See, we can drag her along.

*He puts the **Old Lady** in stretcher.*

*They all pack up the rest of their belongings and start on their journey, pulling the **Old Lady**, possibly using the parachute billowing to signify wind, etc. Music, sounds of weather, etc., as they battle on. Possibly this is a song, Brechtian in style.*

**Soldier**
I stalk the truth.
Wrestle with the wind,
as it thumps and kicks me,

like a moving, twisting wall,
between me and the truth.
My burden of hope weighs heavy,
as I stalk the truth.

**Boy**

I can feel my feet on the path,
blindly stumbling,
thorns tear my clothes,
wind sears my mind.
I charge on to the top,
through the mess,
hoping for a clearing.

**Girl**

Like a leaf,
I'm being carried along.
The wind pushes and pulls
my senses . . . my thoughts
are confused.
Helpless I'll land . . . when it stops
on a track worn down before us.

**Old Lady**

The rain washes my body,
chills my old bones,
prepares me for something,
other than this.
The top is too high,
I'll arrive somewhere else.
The rain pounds me.
Submit, submit, lie down,
your fight is done.

*The* **Soldier** *and* **Boy** *collapse at the same time, exhausted from pulling*

**Soldier** *and* **Boy**

Can't go another step.

**Soldier**

The wind's getting colder.

**Girl**
> Are we going the right way?

**Boy**
> Up is up.

**Soldier**
> I see no marks.

**Boy**
> This isn't a bloody paper trail. No one has marked it out for us in advance.

**Girl**
> How do you know?

**Boy**
> You what?

**Girl**
> That this isn't part of something else, a pattern?

**Boy**
> Oh, I get it, the world fell apart so that the four of us could be together on a bloody cold mountain . . . That explains it all!

*He starts to try and put up shelter in the wind. The* **Soldier** *helps.*

**Soldier**
> I had a weird dream last night . . . about the world . . . us . . . my friend. I was climbing up a huge mountain, it was soft, I kept sinking into it. I was trying to write a song in my head . . . I kept nearly getting it. I stood up, the mountain changed, it was a . . .

*Makes a gesture of a breast.*

> You know.

**Boy**
> You what?

**Soldier**
> You know . . .

**Old Lady**
> Tit . . . he means tit.

**Boy**
> Sick . . . Hold that side tight, will you?

**Soldier**
> I don't mean it like that! . . . I don't know what it means.
> My mate, he was in a boat it was burning, sailing away from
> me. In my dream I knew where he was going . . . I knew . . .
> I can't remember.

**Old Lady**
> I'm going there.

**Soldier**
> Where?

**Old Lady**
> Valhalla . . . it's where the souls of dead heroes go to have a
> good time.

**Boy**
> You what?

**Old Lady**
> If you say 'You what' once more I'll kill you with me bare
> hands!

**Soldier**
> Hag, you're good at riddles . . . What does it mean?

**Old Lady**
> How should I know! It ain't my dream.

**Boy** (*throws down shelter in rage*)
> This is useless, it's not going to stay up.

**Old Lady**
> Just 'cause I'm old don't mean I know everything.

**Boy**
> His dream's about her . . . It's about her.

*He points at the* **Old Lady**. *Everybody looks.*

**Old Lady** (*covering her breasts over*)
Leave me be!

**Girl**
You what?

**Boy**
It's obvious . . . She's slowing us down, making it impossible to get to the top.

**Soldier**
It weren't that . . .

**Girl**
Trust you to find a simple explanation!

**Boy**
You must all see!

**Girl**
How could you?

**Boy**
Because I have to . . . someone does. I want us to have a chance, to make something together.

**Girl**
Like love, you mean?

**Boy**
There's not much hope of that with this lot around? You're all soft . . .

**Soldier**
That ain't what it meant . . . It's like the song. I've nearly got it . . . It's about the world . . . It's not right leaving her . . .

**Boy**
And that head smells, it's driving me mad.

**Soldier**
He's with me.

**Boy**
All these things people won't leave . . . Why don't you bury it?

**Old Lady**

If we're staying here we best get sorted. How much food we got?

**Boy**

You eating again?

*It is raining hard. Sound of wind. All are shivering.*

**Old Lady**

My leg is hot but the rest of me is cold.

**Girl**

We could light a fire.

**Boy**

In this wind?

**Girl**

We could try.

**Boy**

We've no wood.

**Soldier**

I'll find some wood.

**Girl**

I'll come with you.

**Boy**

It doesn't need two of you.

**Girl**

Be quicker.

*The **Soldier** and **Girl** go off.*

*The **Boy**, angry, picks up his knife and starts hacking angrily at wood. The **Old Lady** is quietly sewing. The **Boy** sees the head and threatens it with knife.*

**Boy**

What you looking at . . . ?

*Turns head round.*

**Old Lady**
It's not him you're angry at.

**Boy**
She's changed.

**Old Lady**
People do.

**Boy**
I mean since he came, she's changed. We were together, me and her . . . It's all changing.

**Old Lady**
Things do.

**Boy**
I don't like it.

*He goes to her bag and takes out her diary.*

**Old Lady**
Is that yours?

**Boy**
Go to sleep, old woman.

**Old Lady**
That's thievin'.

**Boy**
Shut it.

*He starts to look through it. He finds what he is looking for.*

You see, here it says she loves my smell, that she feels safe with me.

*Turns a few pages.*

Why's she writing all this crap about the world? Ah, here . . . here she says I'm changing, that she doesn't understand what's happening to me.

*To the* **Old Lady**.

She's the one that's changing . . . not me. You can see that can't you?

**Old Lady**
Part of something.

**Boy**
Why do you talk in riddles?

**Old Lady**
Because they're harder to understand

**Boy**
Flipping mad you are.

**Old Lady**
The truth hurts. Sometimes you need to wrap it up and hold it before you open it.

**Boy**
Do you think she fancies him then? . . . We were perfect till you two came along.

**Old Lady**
We're life.

**Boy**
Death, you mean . . .

*To the* **Old Lady** *and audience.*

How do I do it?
How?

*Waves knife around.*

Before all this she said she loved me.
What's changed?
Apart from the world?
I haven't changed . . . I want her . . . I always have.
She's changed.
I don't feel close to her any more.
One . . . we used to be one.
I know that sounds soft,
but it's true,
I could feel her heart beating at the same time as mine,
we even walk at the same pace,

the same size strides.
Even that's different now,
there's a wall between us,
and she built it.
I didn't . . .
I just want things the way they were.
It's as if things are changing and I can only watch.
I want to pull it all back,
but it keeps going forward . . .

**Old Lady**

Look at me, your girl will look like me one day . . . change
that much . . . I looked like her once. Bet you would of
fancied me.

**Boy** (*embarrassed*)

I . . . I just wanted it to stay the same . . . some people stay
together, people don't change all the time.

**Old Lady**

Things get in the way, interrupt. You can't stay still. People
change, countries change, the world changes. Everything
moves around, then it all finds a different shape . . . a new
pattern.

**Boy** (*looking in the diary again*)

I just want to see if she still loves me . . . this bit is all about
maggot-head and his mate.

*The* **Boy** *is engrossed in the diary. The* **Girl** *comes running in, excited.
The* **Soldier** *follows holding a rabbit.*

**Girl**

We saw a rabbit . . . he caught it.

*She stops when she sees his guilty expression.*

What's wrong?

**Boy** (*hiding the diary behind his back*)

Nothing.

**Girl**

You look guilty.

**Boy**
I said nothing.

**Girl** (*she goes to have a look*)
Come on . . . what is it?

**Boy**
Leave me alone, go and skin your rabbit, you and soldier
boy.

**Girl**
Come on . . . I know you.

**Boy**
Do you?

**Girl**
Yes.

**Boy**
Do you really?

**Girl**
Yes.

**Boy**
Do you love me?

**Girl**
What's that got to do with anything?

*She makes a plunge at him to look behind his back and sees the diary.*

You rat! You stinking rat . . . that's my secret.

**Boy** (*he throws it at her*)
Keep your secrets . . . or share them with two-heads.

**Girl**
You betrayed me . . . I trusted you.

**Boy**
And I did you.

**Girl**
What have I done?

**Boy**
All innocent now are we? Maybe I should ask two-heads.

*He grabs the head, turns to the* **Soldier** *and starts to wind him up by waving the head at him as he chants.*

**Boy**
Stinking, been thinking while you've been gone,
Stinking needs sinking . . .

**Girl** (*tries to grab head*)
Stop it!

**Boy**
Stinking ain't blinking . . .

**Girl**
Stop it!

**Boy**
Stinking ain't thinking or blinking, he's stinking . . .

**Girl**
Stop it, stop it!

*The* **Girl** *manages to get the head. The* **Soldier** *holds the rabbit up and cuts its belly open, blood pours out . . . Silence.*

**Soldier**
I'm going to cook dinner.

*The* **Girl** *places the head in its bag.*

**Old Lady**
The head is the soul, that's why he can't let it go.

**Boy**
He's mental, that's why he can't let it go.

*The* **Girl** *picks up her diary, gives the* **Boy** *a look.*

**Boy**
I just needed to know.

**Girl**
You had no right.

**Boy**
I know.

**Girl**
You were wrong to look.

**Boy**
I was desperate . . .

**Girl**
It means there's no rules and you promised.

**Boy**
Together for ever . . . You promised.

*He storms off. The* **Girl** *sits at the* **Old Lady**'s *feet.*

**Girl**
How's your leg?

**Old Lady**
Hot.

**Girl**
Let's change the dressing.

**Old Lady**
There's no point.

**Girl**
Don't say that . . . Everything just seems to get worse. First there was chaos down there and I got away . . . and now it seems to have come back again here. I feel so confused.

**Old Lady**
Love is confusing.

**Girl**
I never said I belonged.

**Old Lady**
I think if you're in love then you want to belong.

**Girl**
How would you know?

**Old Lady**

I've had a few fellas' arms around me.

**Girl**

What should I do?

**Old Lady**

That's for you . . .

**Girl**

It's getting dark . . . the wind is getting up, everything feels
so threatening . . . It's always worse at night . . . anything
can happen at night.

*The **Soldier** is cooking the rabbit.*

**Soldier**

I felt his life wriggle and stop in my hands,
his warm little body . . . stop.

*The **Girl** helps the **Soldier** who talks to her as he cooks the rabbit.
The **Old Lady** is sewing. The **Boy** arrives at the stream, breathless
and sobbing. He is crying with frustration, kicking the rock. He lies down
and drinks from the stream and washes his face.*

**Boy**

Stop, stop, stop blubbing . . . Cow, cow, cow –

*Starts to shout it louder.*

Cow, cow –

*Sobbing.*

Cow!

*Echo back, he does it again.*

Cow!

*Echo.*

Bitch!

*Echo. He stands on rock and shouts.*

HATE YOU!

*Echo.*

Love you.

*Echo.*

Love you, hate you, love you, hate you.

*Sits on the rock, hugging himself.*

I just want to hold her tight.

**Soldier**
I squeezed the neck tighter and tighter.

**Boy**
I want to spend the rest of my life with her.

**Soldier**
Rang the life out of it.

**Boy**
Sometimes I want her so much, my body hurts. I want to cry out, to beg and plead. But if I do that she'll laugh, but if I don't . . .

**Soldier**
And it mattered.

**Boy**
I want everything to stay the same.

**Soldier**
I took a life, felt it slide out.

**Boy**
I can't look at the world without trembling inside. Whirling and whirling so it makes my head dizzy. If I hold her I can keep still, feel my feet on the ground, stop the world.

**Soldier**
I can't feel like I did before . . . before the war. It's like there's a different brain in there, one full of pictures of broken bodies.

*To the* **Girl***.*

Do you know what people look like when their guts are on the top?

*He points to the rabbit. The* **Girl** *looks away.*

**Soldier**
I can't go back, forget what I saw. I feel like something is broken inside me . . . but I don't know what.

**Boy**
My guts are twisted, they twist and churn specially when she talks to him. I feel like I'm going to stop breathing . . . I want to kill him.

**Soldier**
Daft all this killing.

**Boy**
He don't love her like I do . . . He doesn't understand her. I knew who she was before . . . where she's coming from. She's part of my past and I'm part of hers. I understand what she thinks . . . what she wants . . . I can be tough, a killer –

*Starts to mark his face with mud.*

I can be anything, I'll show her, I'll show them all.

*The* **Girl** *and* **Soldier** *are giggling and flirting as they cook rabbit. The* **Soldier** *tears off a leg.*

**Soldier**
Here, Hag . . . have some rabbit.

**Girl**
Don't call her that.

*The* **Old Lady** *takes the leg and eats with relish.*

**Soldier**
Don't mind, do you, Hag?

**Old Lady**
You shot me, why should I mind a name?

**Girl**
It's not polite. My nan would kill you.

**Old Lady**
It wasn't polite when he shot me . . . but he did.

**Soldier**
It was an accident.

**Old Lady**
Everything's an accident . . . I bet you were an accident.

**Soldier**
Probably.

*The* **Boy** *is covering his face in mud the way soldiers do.*

**Girl**
I hope he's all right.

**Soldier**
Do you?

**Girl**
Of course I do.

**Old Lady**
He's finding this hard.

**Soldier**
Who isn't?

**Old Lady**
I mean love . . .

**Soldier**
He don't know what love is . . . he's just a boy.

**Old Lady**
And you're a man, I suppose.

**Soldier** (*puffs himself up*)
Yes.

**Girl**
Man boy, boy man, what's the difference?

**Old Lady**
Can you thread this?

*Gives the* **Girl** *needle and thread.*

**Old Lady**
My eyes.

**Soldier**
Why you still mending?

**Old Lady**
It helps.

**Soldier**
There's no point.

**Old Lady** (*holding up the quilt*)
Everything's in this, my world . . . What you see?

*She points out.*

**Soldier**
Smoke, black smoke . . .

**Girl**
Can't you see the colours? Over there –

**Soldier**
Blood, a river of blood.

**Girl**
Lava, a roaring red monster of lava swallowing everything
in its path.

**Old Lady**
Heart of the world.

**Soldier**
Mud, just mud.

**Girl**
Clot, a clot of people.

**Old Lady**
Bloodletting.

**Soldier** (*getting excited*)
Raining spears.

**Girl**
And arrows . . . This mountain takes you out of time, you
can see everything of all time together.

**Old Lady**
The edges of time frayed . . .

*The* **Soldier** *pulls some flesh from the rabbit and feeds it to the* **Girl**.
*As he does so, the* **Boy** *runs in breathless and triumphant until he sees
this. He then gets angry.*

**Boy**
You see! Lies, all lies.

**Soldier**
Now what?

**Boy** (*to the* **Girl**)
Nothing you say . . .

**Girl**
What?

**Boy**
Nothing true . . .

**Girl**
What?

**Boy**
Lies . . . all lies . . .

**Girl**
I . . .

**Boy**
Traitor . . . traitor . . .

**Girl**
What do you mean?

**Boy**
Vegetarian, you said you were a vegetarian.

**Soldier** (*laughs*)
This boy's gone.

*Points to head.*

**Girl**
I'm hungry . . . you said it was silly anyway.

**Boy**
It just shows, doesn't it . . . how quickly you change.

**Girl**
Everything's changed . . . I have to, so have you, you look different.

*Touches his face.*

**Boy**
I'm a warrior.

**Soldier** *laughs.*

**Girl**
You see? You said you didn't believe in fighting.

**Boy**
This is for survival.

**Girl**
So is eating.

*The **Boy** takes something out of his pocket and hands it to her.*

**Girl**
What's this?

**Soldier** (*looking over her shoulder*)
Glass?

**Girl** (*she looks at it*)
A piece of mirror . . . you've given me a piece of mirror.

**Soldier** (*sarcastically*)
Really useful.

*The **Girl** silences him with a look.*

**Boy**
You said . . .

**Girl**
Thank you . . .

**Boy**
I . . .

**Girl**
Really appreciate it . . .

**Boy**
A token . . .

*She gives him a kiss.*

**Soldier**
Will I get a kiss if I find you a piece of glass?

**Girl**
Where did you find it?

**Boy**
Down.

**Girl**
You went down there for me?

**Soldier**
What's it like now?

**Boy**
Hell.

**Girl**
Brave.

**Soldier**
Bloody daft.

*The* **Boy** *turns on the* **Soldier**.

**Soldier**
OK, OK.

**Boy** (*to the* **Girl**)

It's all getting closer. The air is getting choked. Any left will suffocate soon. We need to move further up, so we can breathe.

*He puts his arm around her.*

We'll go to the top . . . start again, Adam and Eve.

**Girl**

We can't leave them, I told you . . . that's wrong. It can't be just the two of us . . . not now.

**Boy**

Why not?

*The* **Old Lady** *shows the* **Girl** *a patch in the quilt.*

**Girl**

That's like my skirt.

**Old Lady**

Hope of the world.

**Boy**

Do I get any of this rabbit?

*The* **Girl** *plays with the mirror. The* **Old Lady** *starts to hum a lullaby. The* **Girl** *goes over to her.*

**Girl**

You look tired.

*She and the* **Old Lady** *make a bed and climb into it. Both the* **Boy** *and the* **Soldier** *spot this.*

**Boy** (*acting casual, stretches*)

I'm tired . . . I think I'll go to bed.

**Soldier**

Me too.

*They both move towards the bed. The* **Soldier** *is nearer.*

**Boy**

The fire's not out.

**Soldier**
So?

**Boy**
It's your turn.

**Soldier**
Since when have there been turns?

**Boy**
Now, and it's yours.

**Soldier**
You're nearest.

**Boy**
I put the last piece of wood on.

**Soldier**
Oh dear.

**Boy**
Go on then.

**Soldier**
I caught the rabbit.

**Boy**
That doesn't count.

**Soldier**
I'm going to bed.

**Boy**
Let's put it out together.

**Soldier**
Get lost!

*The* **Soldier** *heads towards bed. The* **Boy** *charges in front of him and bars his way.*

**Boy**
She's my girl. I sleep next to her.

**Soldier**
Who says?

**Boy**
  I do.

*They face each other. The **Old Lady**'s lullaby gets louder.*

**Boy**
  Shut that row up.

**Soldier**
  She's all right.

**Boy**
  You say? I didn't shoot her.

**Girl**
  I've had enough . . . Here!

*She changes places so that the first one in will be next to the **Old Lady**. Now they become very polite, letting the other go first. Eventually the **Boy** concedes and gets into bed. They all settle down. The **Soldier** sneaks the head into the bed.*

**Boy** (*screams*)
  There's something slimy on my feet.

*He dives out and looks at foot of bed. He pulls out the head.*

  It's maggot-head.

*He starts to brush the bed as if brushing away maggots.*

**Soldier**
  Oh, go to sleep.

**Boy**
  Why did you have to put that in here?

*He chucks the head away.*

**Soldier**
  I thought he'd get cold.

**Boy**
  He's already cold, dead cold.

*The **Soldier** snatches the blanket and goes off to sleep somewhere else with the head. He talks to the head.*

**Soldier**
> Deadhead, my friend's a deadhead.
> Always talking, 'e was,
> quiet now.
> Deadhead, my friend's a deadhead.

> Make a good song that.

*The others are sleeping restlessly. Loud explosion. They all panic. The* **Boy** *finds his knife, the* **Soldier** *his gun.*

**Old Lady** (*starts shaking her fists and yelling*)
> Still trying, are we? . . . 'Ere I am, then . . . Come on.

**Boy** (*shouting*)
> Behind the wall . . . get behind the wall.

*The* **Girl** *and* **Boy** *dive behind the wall.*

**Old Lady**
> Me leg's got it . . . mind you, that was point-blank range
> and I was sitting still.

**Soldier** (*dives at her and pulls her behind the wall*)
> Stupid Hag . . . what you think you're doing?

**Old Lady**
> Dying.

**Boy** (*peering over wall*)
> I told you, didn't I? I told you . . . we should have gone faster.

**Soldier**
> Keep your head down . . . Head . . . Deadhead . . .

*He looks over wall. The head is still where he left it. He starts to go and get it.*

**Boy**
> You can't go out there.

**Girl**
> He's all right.

**Boy**
> It's not going to get killed.

*The* **Soldier** *uses his gun to try and pull the head towards him.*

**Old Lady**
You'll never get it like that.

*She gets up and walks over to the head.*

Who'll take this old hag's life?

**Girl**
Come back.

**Boy**
Don't be daft!

*As she reaches the head there is a loud explosion. The others duck.*

**Old Lady**
More to the right.

*She turns and walks back to the wall with the head. As she reaches the wall there is another explosion which throws her off her feet. She crawls behind the wall. All goes quiet; the noise can still be heard, but further away. They start tentatively to look over the wall. The noise is still loud enough to create tension.*

**Soldier**
They've moved over.

**Boy**
I told you, didn't I? We could have died. If you'd listened to me we'd be at the top by now.

*To the* **Old Lady**.

We can't manage you . . . you're holding us up.

**Girl**
Stop it.

**Boy**
It's the truth . . . face the truth . . . we can't just hold on to things.

**Girl**
Stop it!

**Boy**

You can't, can you? . . . You can't face up to reality . . . That apple blossom you saw . . . remember . . . on a red rug?

*The* **Girl** *puts her hands over her ears.*

**Boy**

White sheets over bodies, hundreds of them . . . it wasn't a bloody picnic, it was a massacre. I'm not rearranging reality to suit, I'm looking at it straight in the face . . . talking the truth. We can't hold on to things regardless.

**Girl**

What about responsibility? What about caring? You don't just let go of things because it suits.

**Boy**

What about survival? All of you won't let go . . . you're all hanging on to things.

**Old Lady**

Life's hanging on to to me.

**Boy**

That bloody quilt . . . like carting a dead dog around.

**Old Lady**

And you don't hold on to anything I suppose . . . I've heard you: 'Change . . . I don't like change.'

**Boy**

It's not the same as holding on to a maggot-head.

*Fetches head and holds it up to the* **Soldier**.

Let go of it . . . Now!

**Soldier**

Don't do that.

**Boy**

Bury it . . . Come on . . . I'll bury it for you . . . dig a hole.

**Soldier**

No!

**Boy**
It'd be best.

**Soldier**
I can't.

**Boy**
Hygienic.

**Soldier**
He's not dirty.

**Boy**
Just rotting.

**Soldier**
Leave it . . . It's not time.

**Boy**
It's ripe enough . . . Come on, put it in the ground where it belongs.

*He starts to dig a hole with his heel, daring the* **Soldier**. *The* **Soldier** *grabs his gun.*

**Soldier**
Put it down.

**Boy** (*takes out his knife*)
Make me.

*They face each other.*

**Girl**
Why did the war have to come here?

**Boy** (*to the* **Girl**)
Stand behind me.

**Girl**
No!

**Boy**
Whose side you on?

*The* **Old Lady** *stands between the the* **Boy** *and the* **Soldier**.

**Old Lady**
Come on then, between the two of you, might manage it.
Aim the knife at me heart. Keep the gun up, Sonny.

**Soldier**
Get out the way, Hag.

**Old Lady**
I'm the target.

**Boy**
I don't want to hurt you.

**Old Lady** (*to the* **Boy**)
You want to kill 'im, do you?

**Boy**
Self-defence.

**Old Lady** (*to the* **Soldier**)
You want to kill 'im?

**Soldier**
Defence.

**Old Lady**
Right's on my side, that's what they all say. That's why it
never ends.

**Girl**
You don't have to know why you hold on to things, reasons
only part of it . . . She's right . . . You're always trying to
keep things the same . . . Hold on to me . . . stop things
changing.

*She takes the head and hands it to the* **Soldier**.

**Boy**
'Cause I'm scared.

**Girl**
We're all scared . . . we all hold on to things.

**Soldier**
I'll let go when it feels right.

**Boy**
She's old. It's hard but it's true.

**Girl**
No!

**Old Lady**
To hold on to anything is hard, like holding a monkey. I don't want you or life to hold on to me. You see things as burdens, maybe they're gifts.

**Boy**
You make me feel like the enemy. I'm just being practical.

**Soldier**
We ain't leaving her . . . I can carry her.

**Boy**
There's been enough dying, but if some of us can survive then surely that's better than none.

**Soldier**
I can carry her.

**Boy**
Have you seen how steep it is?

**Soldier**
I'll stay here.

**Boy**
Fine.

**Old Lady**
No one is staying on my account.

**Soldier**
I can't leave you.

**Old Lady**
We all have to die sometime . . . here feels fine.

**Girl**
Don't say that.

**Old Lady**
> Listen . . . I can't come with you and if you stay here you'll
> die as well. What's the good in that?

**Girl**
> But . . .

**Old Lady**
> I can't be doing with interruptions.

*They wrap her in a blanket. The* **Girl** *starts to cry.*

**Soldier**
> I should stay and defend you, that's what soldiers are for.

**Old Lady**
> Well, stop being a soldier then and defend yourself. You
> young people think you're the only ones who can do
> anything . . .

*The* **Girl** *kneels next to the* **Old Lady***. The* **Soldier** *and* **Boy** *pack
up.*

**Old Lady**
> I'm on the edge of life,
> opening the last door.

**Girl**
> There's a door in my dreams.

**Old Lady**
> The last bit's as hard as the first.
> I thought death would be easy,
> I would slide through death's door like a blade on ice.

**Girl**
> There's glass but it's distorted,
> making patterns and colours.

**Old Lady**
> No glass in this door, blank,
> is this it? Nothing behind?
> Or is the best left to last?
> A surprise.

**Girl**

> I want to hurl myself at the door,
> rush into the next bit.

**Old Lady**

> I will let go of the thread slowly . . . my last breath.

**Girl**

> Each door.

**Old Lady**

> A change.

**Girl**

> Full of patterns. I want to move in, I know I can.

**Old Lady**

> Do doors change to windows
> with clear glass
> after death?
> One looking onto the next endlessly.
> Or are there curtains to swish
> with the ease of the dead?

**Girl**

> I can see myself in the door,
> sort of,
> misshapen,
> changing.

**Old Lady**

> Death reflects no images,
> the change is complete.

*They get ready to leave, the* **Girl** *sobbing and looking behind.*

**Girl**

> I love you.

**Old Lady**

> Get going . . .

**Boy**

> Ready . . . forward . . .

*Tries to be casual.*

Bye then.

**Old Lady**
See you on the other side.

**Boy** (*still casual*)
I'm off . . . all the best.

**Old Lady**
Goodbye.

**Boy**
See you.

**Old Lady**
Goodbye.

*The three go onward, and reach a steep bit of ledge. The* **Boy** *steps onto the ledge and with difficulty heaves himself up very slowly, nearly slipping. The* **Girl** *is pinned against the ledge; she doesn't like heights. During this scene the* **Old Lady** *is singing her 'Sewing Song' (see page 72) quietly.*

**Soldier**
Don't look down.

**Girl**
I can't help it.

**Soldier**
Here, take my hand.

**Girl**
I can't move.

**Soldier**
Slowly.

**Boy** (*shouts down*)
What's going on down there?

**Soldier**
Coming!

**Girl**
You go.

**Soldier**
Look, just take my hand.

**Girl** (*puts out her hand*)
I can't reach.

**Soldier** (*moves back towards her*)
There . . .

*He takes her hand.*

Now keep your eyes level with mine.

**Girl**
I keep wanting to see.

**Soldier**
Don't.

**Boy**
What are you doing down there?

**Soldier**
It's all right!

**Boy**
You leave my girl alone.

**Soldier**
Shut it! That's it, you're doing fine.

**Boy**
I'm coming back down!

**Soldier** (*to the* **Boy**)
Stop being so bloody silly!

*To the* **Girl**.

Now, go behind me, keep looking at me.

**Girl** (*sobbing*)
I feel sick.

**Soldier**
Nearly there . . . you're great.

**Girl**
My legs.

**Soldier**
Just keep going.

**Boy**
Stop leaving me out, what you two doing?

**Soldier**
There, now . . . ready!

**Boy**
Hallelujah!

*He lies on his stomach, puts his hands over the cliff and waits for the* **Girl** *to reach a point where he can help pull her up.*

There!

**Girl** (*shaking*)
I don't like this.

**Old Lady**
My journey begins.

**Boy** (*to the* **Soldier**)
You ready?

*The* **Soldier** *starts to climb.*

**Boy** (*to the* **Girl**)
What were you doing down there?

**Girl**
What do you mean?

**Boy**
You were a long time.

**Girl**
I was scared . . . What you saying?

**Boy**
I don't feel close to you.

**Girl**
There's not time . . .

**Boy**
I need to . . .

**Girl**
We shouldn't have left her.

**Boy**
We had to.

**Girl**
We killed her.

**Boy**
We would have died.

**Girl**
I feel responsible.

**Boy**
So do I . . . but we had to.

**Soldier** (*shouts*)
The foothold's gone.

**Boy** (*shouts down but not really listening*)
Find another one . . .

*To the* **Girl**.

I did it for you.

**Soldier** (*sounding worried*)
I can't find one.

**Boy** (*to the* **Soldier**)
Keep looking . . .

*To the* **Girl**.

We deserve a chance.

**Soldier** (*desperate*)
Help!

**Boy**
The two of us . . .

**Soldier**
HELP!

**Boy** (*to the* **Soldier**)
How . . . ?

*To the* **Girl***.*

Do you understand?

**Girl**
Help him, for God's sake.

**Boy**
What can I do ?

**Soldier**
I can't hold for much longer.

**Girl**
Do something.

**Boy** (*very calm*)
Are you losing your grip?

**Soldier**
Yes.

**Boy** (*makes a decision*)
Here . . .

*He leans over and grabs the* **Soldier***'s hand. They hold tight for a moment.*

. . . now keep climbing.

*Then the head falls out of the bag and rolls down the mountain.*

**Soldier**
Deadhead!

**Boy**
Leave him!

**Soldier**
Deadhead!

**Boy**
Come on!

**Soldier**
Deadhead!

**Boy**
I can't hold you . . . keep climbing.

**Girl**
Forget him.

**Soldier**
No!

**Girl**
Please . . .

**Soldier**
This ain't for me . . .

**Girl**
You're nearly there.

**Boy**
I can't . . .

**Soldier**
There's things to put right.

**Girl**
You might die.

**Soldier**
It's a different edge,
the outline ends here for me.

*The* **Soldier** *goes back down. The* **Boy** *and* **Girl** *watch.*

**Girl**
I can't see him.

**Boy**
I feel dizzy.

**Girl**
> Lie down.

*They both lie down on their backs again. The* **Soldier** *reaches the* **Old Lady**, *places the head with her, then covers them over.*

**Soldier**
> Good journey.

*The* **Soldier** *starts to hum or sing very quietly during the couple's next dialogue. This builds so that when they have finished he is in full song. The couple move back behind wall and the* **Soldier** *exits. (Metallica's 'Through the Never' would fit perfectly.)*

**Girl**
> They put a watch into a spaceship and sent it hurtling round the earth. When it arrived back the watch they'd left behind was faster.

**Boy**
> What was the point of that?

**Girl**
> To prove that the faster you go the slower time goes . . .
> I told you!

**Boy**
> You think they'd have better things to do.

**Girl**
> Does being in love make you dizzy or is it the world?

**Boy**
> Like running on a football.

**Girl**
> It feels like we've been here for ever.

**Boy**
> Will we be together for ever?

**Girl**
> I don't know . . . there's more than one pattern.

## Old Lady's Sewing Song

Belfast, Basra, Biafra, Flanders, Bengal, Dagestan,
Waterloo, Estonia, Berlin, Hiroshima, Tiananmen Square,
Lithuania, Derry, Agincourt, Croatia, Hastings.

Pull the world through the eye of a needle.
Pierce the skin of the world.
Mend the breach.
Broken lines redefine.
Push pull,
mend and heal.
The sea breaks here . . . build a wall.
The people mass there, prevent a fall.
Tightly, tightly I must sew this bit tightly.
The fabric is threadbare, it will take all my skill.
Carefully, carefully.
Make patterns from chaos.
Warm wool, cold shroud, black crepe, white cape.
Two become one, the join does not show.
Once was a wall now a seam.
Together, together I must seal them together,
hide the scar.
It's hard mending the world.
Push pull,
mend and heal.
Azerbaijan, Aquitaine, Latvia, Krishnapur, Catalonia,
Kuwait, Palestine . . .

# The Raft

*The Raft* was produced by BBC Radio 4 and was first broadcast on 27 May 2002. The cast was as follows:

| | |
|---|---|
| **Mags** | Annabelle Dowler |
| **Soul** | Inika Leigh Wright |
| **Goaler 1/Submariner** | Tyrone Huggins |
| **Gaoler 2/Ugly Mermaid** | Sunny Ormonde |
| **Chorus 1** | Gillian Goodman |
| **Chorus 2** | Bella Merlin |
| **Chorus 3** | Tracey Briggs |

*Director/Producer*    Peter Leslie Wild

## Characters

**Mags**, *a young frail girl about eighteen, withdrawing from heroin, with a three-year-old son. She is in prison for stealing*

**Soul**, *Mags' soul, frail and nervous, terrified of the salt water, wants to hang on and not drown in the sea*

**Gaoler 1 / Submariner**, *middle-aged man. Wise, kind and concerned for the prisoners, has a warm deep voice*

**Gaoler 2 / Ugly Mermaid**, *middle-aged woman. Has no time for the prisoners, seen it all too many times, is hardened to their plight*

**Chorus of Shrouds 1**, *2*, **3**, *all women. Three voices: usually only one voice speaks at a time unless marked for all. They are Mags' destiny of fear and dread, but there is also a sense of humour about them. Chorus 1 is the more serious of the three voices*

## Scene One

*The setting: a prison.*

*The sounds of a prison, doors banging and being locked. The hollow echoey sound of voices and the sounds of women wailing and banging on their doors which gradually, almost imperceptibly, turns to the sound of the sea. The sea gets louder and wilder until all we hear are crashing waves and a storm. Over this comes the quiet gentle singing of Jeff Buckley singing the first riffs of 'Hallelujah'.*

## Scene Two

*The prison.*

*We are with* **Mags** *in her cell. Outside are the sounds of the prison: the echoey shouting, banging of bars, the odd desperate forlorn shout from women in cells.*

**Mags** *is struggling to keep herself calm. Sitting on her bed, thin and weak, suffering from withdrawal, she is shaking as she struggles to talk herself out of panic and despair. She is looking at a photo of her son Robbie.*

**Mags**
If I listen . . .

*Pause.*

If I listen real hard, I can hear him.

*Pause as we hear the sounds of the prison.*

If I listen,
If I listen real hard, I can hear his sweet little voice.
And I can hold on.

*Trying to convince herself.*

I can hold on to that.

*Pause.*

I can trace his little fat face round this photo.

I can touch his smile.
I can hear his voice.

*Pause as she listens to the bleak sounds of the prison, the wailing and the banging and the echoey sounds outside her cell.*

But then his voice gets lost,
lost in me head.

*Slight rising panic.*

And the sea starts,
and this creaking and groaning,
and the shrouds we've been stitchin' start singing me songs.

*Resigned.*

Then I know,
I know that I can't,
that I just can't hold on.

*The sounds of the prison are heard.*

**Gaoler 1** (*shouts down the corridor*)
Behind your doors, behind your doors.

*We hear* **Gaoler 1** *whistle 'Bobby Shaftoe' as he walks down the corridor. We fade into a body-count in Scene Three.*


## Scene Three

*The prison.*

*A body-count by* **Gaoler 1** *is heard down the corridor of the prison; this has a rhythmic feel to it. It is heard coming closer. Very faintly underneath this is the sound of the sea (a sluggish, heavy sea like the Dead Sea, heavy waves lapping slowly). As* **Gaoler 1** *locks doors we hear faintly the sounds of women wailing, shouting and banging on the doors.*

**Gaoler 1**
One in.

*The door is slammed shut and locked.*

*He walks along the corridor a bit, at regular intervals the sound of his keys jangling, the odd burst of whistling.*

*He stops to look into a cell. He shouts.*

Two in.

*The door is slammed and locked.*

*He walks again. He stops, looks in. Shouts.*

One in.

*The door is slammed and locked.*

*He walks again. Whistles to himself. He stops looks in. Shouts.*

Two in.

*All the time* **Gaoler 1** *is getting closer to* **Mags**' *cell. As he gets closer we hear the sound of the sea underneath getting very slightly louder.*

One in.

*The door is slammed and locked.* **Gaoler 1** *walks closer. The sea sound gets a little louder. He reaches the cell and looks in. He shouts with alarm.*

Jesus Christ!

*The sound of the sea is now a little clearer.*

*He is trying to sound calm.*

What you doing up there, lassie?
You don't want to be up there.

*Shouts down the corridor.*

Need a hand over here, we've got a problem.

*To* **Mags** *from doorway: reasoning, trying to keep her calm.*

Come on now, Mags, what you doing standing on your bed?

**Mags** (*urgently*)
Don't come in.

**Gaoler 1** (*gently*)
It's not good for you up there.

**Mags** (*urgently*)
Don't come in, you'll drown.

**Gaoler 1** (*humouring her*)
Don't worry about me, I know how to swim.

**Mags**
The water's deep.

**Gaoler 1**
You don't say.

**Mags**
Leave me alone!

**Gaoler 1**
Not with that noose round your neck I can't.

**Mags**
Tell Robbie I'm sorry.

**Gaoler 2** (*arrives, breathless*)
What is it? What's going on?

**Gaoler 1**
Trying to take herself off.

**Gaoler 2** (*annoyed*)
Not another one.

**Mags** (*explains*)
Tell Robbie I'm sorry, But there's a noise in me head. All this creaking and groaning. And the shrouds we've been stitchin' keep singing me songs.

**Gaoler 2**
Sometimes I think they make more sense when they're on drugs than when their coming off 'em.

**Mags**
Tell Robbie I'm sorry, I tried to hold on.

**Gaoler 1**
You can tell him yourself come visiting day.

**Gaoler 2** (*firmly*)
You're not going anywhere.

**Gaoler 1** (*enters the cell*)
I'll lift her down.

*Removes the noose.*

You won't be needing that round your neck.

*Picks her up*

There we are.

*Thinks to himself.*

She's like a small bird,
shot through the heart.

*To* **Mags**.

Down you come.

**Gaoler 2** (*practical*)
Best get her to the sui-cell.

**Gaoler 1**
She's like a child.

**Gaoler 2**
She has a child of her own.

**Gaoler 1**
Come on, girl, let's put you somewhere safe.

**Gaoler 2**
We don't want to lose another one.


**Scene Four**

*The sea.*

*A sea, dark and heavy, lapping slowly. A raft creaks with the weight of its burden on the sea. On the raft lie the corpses of the dead and dying, moaning and wailing (the same sound as in the prison). Seagulls call and hover overhead. A gentle wind flaps the sails and shrouds. We hear the* **Chorus** *of the sails and shrouds.*

**Chorus 1**
> We are the chorus of shrouds
> that shrift in the winds of her mind.

**Chorus 2**
> We are the chorus of shrouds,
> singing her songs of the sea.

**Chorus 3**
> We are the destiny of many,
> a chorus of fear and despair.

**All Chorus**
> The raft of Medusa.

**Scene Five**

*The prison.*

**Mags** *is being carried to the sui-cell. We hear the prison sounds of women banging on their doors, wailing and yelling. A cell door is opened and we hear the keys on the* **Gaolers'** *waistbands jangling.* **Gaoler 1** *and* **2** *put* **Mags** *into the sui-cell.*

**Gaoler 1**
> Here we are, love, you'll be safe in here.

**Gaoler 2**
> Put her on the mattress.

*Starts to undress her.*

> I'll get her into this gear.

**Gaoler 1** (*to* **Gaoler 2**)
> She's all bones and gooseflesh.

**Gaoler 2**
> That's why they call it cold turkey.

**Gaoler 1**
> I guess the vomiting will start soon.

**Gaoler 2**

And the muscle spasms.

**Gaoler 1**

She's going to tear that to shreds.

**Gaoler 2**

At least she won't be able to hang herself with it.

**Gaoler 1**

These girls wear their destiny like an albatross.

**Gaoler 2**

You're too soft for this place, see things in pictures. It's fact we deal with here.

**Gaoler 1**

So what fact is this lying here?

**Gaoler 2**

A serial shoplifter with a drug problem.

**Gaoler 1**

And a child, with a child. How does a girl get to this state?

**Gaoler 2**

Lack of direction is tattooed on the soul.

**Gaoler 1**

But it's hard to find your way sometimes.

**Gaoler 2**

We all have to push forward, follow the signs. Stick to the route. Not go round in circles. Once you've got lost . . .

**Gaoler 1**

Easy to say if you're born with a map. If the signposts are clear.

**Gaoler 2**

We come into this world in a sack, and depart in another. What happens in between is up to us.

**Gaoler 1**

You've no soul?

**Gaoler 2**
  I didn't need it.

**Mags** (*feebly*)
  Is this it?

**Gaoler 2**
  Is this what?

**Mags**
  The end?

**Gaoler 1**
  She doesn't even know where she is.

**Gaoler 2**
  They never do when they're coming off smack.

**Mags** (*suddenly, urgently*)
  Where's me picture, me picture of Robbie?

**Gaoler 1**
  I'll fetch it later.

**Gaoler 2**
  Best not.

**Gaoler 1**
  She can't harm herself with a photo.

**Gaoler 2**
  You never know with this lot, slash themselves with a paper bag given half the chance.

**Gaoler 1**
  If I bring the photo down it'll give her something to think about.

**Gaoler 2**
  We're here to keep them locked up, not play nursemaid to their minds.

**Gaoler 1**
  We best keep fifteen-minute watch.

*The sound of the sea creeps in.*

**Gaoler 1** (*thinks to himself*) She's looks so frail.

**Mags**
    I'm fallin'.

*The cell door is slammed shut and locked.*


## Scene Six

*The sea.*

*The raft creaks along the sea, heavy with its burden. The shroud/sails flap gently in the breeze. Seagulls call overhead.*

**Chorus 1**
    There is a moment.

**All Chorus**
    Our moment.

**Chorus 1**
    When the dark sea of the unconscious breaks in,
    and the mind
    drops
    into the sea.
    The sea of dread.

**Chorus 3** (*bitterly*)
    A bloody tedious place to be.

**Chorus 2**
    Don't you start moaning again.

**Chorus 3**
    All this creaking and groaning, it's more than a shroud can bear.

**Chorus 1**
    Just be grateful you're not a soul.

## Scene Seven

*The prison.*

*The Judas hole slides open with a loud snap.* **Gaoler 1** *looks in. A moment of silence as he looks at her.*

**Gaoler 1** (*to* **Mags**, *as he looks in the Judas hole*)
    I'll look in again soon.

*The Judas hole is snapped shut. As it shuts . . .*

**Chorus 1**
    And the mind
    drops
    into the sea.
    The sea of dread.


## Scene Eight

*The sea.*

*There is a sudden loud splash as* **Mags** *is dropped into the sea. She gasps with the shock of the cold water and is then pulled under by a small, heavy, sluggish wave. As she resurfaces she gasps again, struggling to keep afloat. Another wave pulls her under. We hear her under the water and then she resurfaces again, gasping for air.*

**Mags**
    Shite!

*She gasps for air and is pulled under again, this time being dragged down deeper. The water starts to sound calmer. Then a surge and she resurfaces again.*

**Mags** (*spluttering and gasping for air*)
    Shite!

*She goes under again, and after a struggle resurfaces.*

**Mags** (*spluttering and gasping*)
    Bag o' shite!

**Soul** (*whispering: a strange ethereal voice*)
Swim.

**Mags** *goes under again and then resurfaces, gasping for air.*

**Soul** (*whispering*)
Swim.

**Mags** (*struggling in the water*)
No.

**Soul** (*more urgently*)
Swim.

**Mags**
Why should I?

**Soul** (*firmly*)
Come on, girl, swim.

**Mags**
I don' wanna.

**Soul**
Save yourself.

**Mags**
What for? Why should I wanna?


**Scene Nine**

*The sea.*

*The raft creaks and drifts slowly through the heavy sea. The seagulls call overhead, the sails flap slightly, the wailing of the dead and dying is heard quietly.*

**Chorus 1**
Once a proud ship set sail from that mind,
its canvas full swell.
But there were no maps,
the waters uncharted.
With no care in the winds,

her ship became calmed.
Stuck.
Drifted to rocks,
shipwrecked.

**Chorus 2**
Society the wrecker,
feeds us our prey.

**Chorus 3**
Her soul clings,
it clings to a mattress.

**Chorus 1**
We can wait,
we'll drift slowly.
The heaviness of our wake will toss the soul in.


**Scene Ten**

*The sea.*

**Mags** *is drifting in the sea. She cares little where she is. Her* **Soul***, perched on the edge of the mattress, is trying to coax her onto the mattress. The only sound is of the heavy lapping of the sea.*

**Soul** (*holding out a hand for her*)
Heave yourself on. Come up here with me.

**Mags** (*sees the mattress*)
It's a mattress, it's a friggin' mattress.

**Soul**
Take hold.

**Mags**
What friggin' good will that be?

**Soul**
It's better than nothin'.

**Mags**
A manky old mattress? It's worse than nothin'.

**Soul**
But we can cling on together.

**Mags**
For what?

**Soul**
Hope.

**Mags** (*starting to drift away in the heavy, slow waves*)
I just wanna sink,
sink deep in this sea.

**Soul**
You can't. It's too soon.

**Mags** (*has drifted further away*)
How do you know?

**Soul** (*calling to her*)
That picture, on your arm.

**Mags** (*still drifting away*)
My tattoo?

**Soul**
Still vibrant with colour.

**Mags**
That's only skin deep.
I've no care to cling.

**Soul**
So you'll drift, be carried away by currents.

**Mags**
Reckon I'll drown in time.

**Soul**
It's hard to drown,
in a sea
heavy with dread.

**Mags**
Living was hard.

**Soul**
    Don't put so much water between you and your soul.

**Mags** (*further away, but still in hailing distance*)
    So come with me.

**Soul**
    There are places a soul don't wanna go.


**Scene Eleven**

*The sea.*

*The raft creaks and heaves its way through the sea, its sail/shrouds flapping slightly, the seagulls calling. The sounds of wailing and moaning are heard slightly.*

**Chorus 1**
    White bones
    jib
    'gainst the grey.

*Pause.*

    Sea-crows perch our top –

*Pause.*

    Dead eyes fix our shrouds –

*Pause.*

    And a wind steers our course.
    Past the shipwrecks of other minds
    drift,
    heavily,
    towards abandoned hope,
    afloat in the sea of dread.

**Chorus 2**
    But her soul clings,
    it clings to a mattress.

**Chorus 3** (*enthusiastically*)
   I could shoot it through the heart
   with my crossbow.

**Chorus 2**
   Don't you dare!

**Chorus 1** (*firmly*)
   We'll wait,
   drift slowly.
   The heaviness of our wake will toss the soul in.


## Scene Twelve

*The sea.*

**Mags** *is still drifting in the heavy sea. Gentle, heavy waves lap around her. When she moves the water splashes. She is getting further away from her* **Soul***.*

**Soul** (*shouts, a long way away*)
   Don't leave me!

*Whines.*

   You just can't leave me like this.

**Mags** (*to herself*)
   This sea is so heavy.

**Soul** (*even further away, pathetically shouting*)
   I don't like it out here,
   on me own,
   all that sea.

**Mags** (*to herself*)
   I thought dying would be lighter.

**Soul**
   All that salt,
   you have to come back.
   I'll end up preserved like a leg of salt beef.

**Mags**
I thought dying would be white.

**Soul** ( *pathetically shouting*)
S.O.S.


## Scene Thirteen

*The prison.*

**Gaoler 1** *is heard walking towards the cell door. We hear the normal prison sounds and his distinctive whistling. He slams open the Judas hole and peers in. A moment of silence.*

**Gaoler 1** (*as he peers into the Judas hole*)
Still with us then, Maggie?

*Concerned.*

You look parched, like a cuttlefish bleached by the sun.

*He unlocks the door and goes in. The sound of the sea comes in and plays quietly underneath.*

**Gaoler 1**
I've brought you some water.

**Mags**
You're walking on water.

**Gaoler 1** ( *joke*)
Didn't anyone tell you?

*He holds the water to her lips.*

Here, drink this, lass.

**Gaoler 2** *arrives and walks in.*

**Gaoler 2** (*briskly*)
How's she doing?

**Gaoler 1**
Her body contorts like the dance of the dead.

**Gaoler 2**

She's kicking the habit.

**Gaoler 1**

There's a sad irony in that butterfly tattooed on her arm.

**Gaoler 2** (*cynical*)

For someone lacking direction.

**Gaoler 1**

A desire for wings.

**Gaoler 2**

Remember Icarus.

**Gaoler 1**

Such a waste of a beautiful young girl.

**Gaoler 2**

That's what they all say: 'What a waste.'
'It shouldn't of happened.' When you've seen it as often as
I have you just think . . . 'It is.'

**Mags**

I'm drifting.

*The sea becomes slightly louder.*


## Scene Fourteen

*The sea.*

*The heavy raft creaks. The sound of the seagulls calling, the sails flapping and the moan of the corpses.*

**Chorus 1**

Our shrouds butt the winds
as the bitumen mast bubbles and blackens
and the corpses of memory,
consigned to fragments,
lie,
shattered and lifeless.

**Chorus 2**
Society the wrecker
feeds us our prey.

*The whizzing sound of a crossbow is heard and then the cry of a shot seagull which falls into the sea.*

**Chorus 1**
What did you do that for?

**Chorus 3**
Target practice.

**Chorus 2**
What had it done to you?

**Chorus 3**
All seagulls are vermin.

**Chorus 1** (*calls, looking out*)
She's drifting towards us.

**Chorus 2**
And her soul still clings.

**Chorus 3** (*sinister*)
Not for long.

**Chorus 1** (*firmly*)
Behave yourself.

**Scene Fifteen**

*The sea.*

**Mags** *is still drifting in the heavy sea. No sounds except the heavy lapping of the waves and the faint sound of her* **Soul** *calling her.*

**Soul** (*whinging from far away*)
Whoever heard of a salted soul?

**Mags** (*thinks*)
The end must be somewhere.

**Soul** (*even fainter*)
    I'm scared.
    It's not right.
    Me soul-teeth are chattering,
    and me sinews are shivering.
    You can't leave me alone,
    a soul all alone,
    in the dark of the night.

**Mags**
    My body aches.

**Soul** (*desperate*)
    So how about –

*She shouts.*

    S.T.S. Save *this* soul!


**Scene Sixteen**

*The sea.*

*The raft creaks closer, its sail flapping. Corpses wail, seagulls call.*

**Chorus 1**
    On lookout.

**Chorus 2**
    The first dogwatch.

**Chorus 3**
    That beat before dawn.

**Chorus 1**
    When the mind sinks,
    and lifelines snap.
    We know we'll make a catch on this cusp of the hours
    when the despair of the day meets the black of the night.

**Chorus 2**
    And the mind takes no more.

**Chorus 3**
Living is not necessary but navigation is.


**Scene Seventeen**

*The sea.*

**Mags** *drifts on in the thick heavy sea. Suddenly an* **Ugly Mermaid** *appears from under the sea in front of* **Mags**.

**Ugly Mermaid**
I smell a lack of direction.

**Mags**
I'm looking for the end.

**Ugly Mermaid**
End of the line?
End of the rainbow?
End of what?

**Mags**
The end of this.

**Ugly Mermaid**
Dread has no end.

**Mags**
How would you know?

**Ugly Mermaid**
Mermaids know everything.

**Mags**
I thought mermaids were beautiful.

**Ugly Mermaid**
Not in the deep dark unconscious.

**Mags**
I feel sick.

**Ugly Mermaid**
All that salt water.

## Scene Eighteen

*The prison.*

**Gaoler 1** *strolls up to the Judas hole, whistling 'Bobby Shaftoe'.*
*Sharply he slides the Judas hole open to look in on* **Mags***. Beat of*
*silence as he looks. The smell of sweat hits him.*

**Gaoler 1**
Blimey, love! Like a sweat-box in there. I could salt herrings.

*Pause.*

Wouldn't you be better on the mattress?


## Scene Nineteen

*The sea.*

*The sound of the creaking raft starts to be heard as it comes closer. The*
*seagulls call and the sails flap. The wailing is getting a little louder,*
*similar to the sound in the prison but slightly different.*

**Chorus 1**
So we drift nearer this newly wrecked mind.

**Ugly Mermaid**
Here comes your destiny right on time.

**Mags**
What is it?

**Chorus 2**
With our shriftering shrouds.

**Ugly Mermaid**
A raft.

**Chorus 1**
Singing her songs.

**Mags**
Full of corpses.

**Chorus 2**
Songs of the sea.

**Ugly Mermaid**
They're not all dead.

**Mags**
You mean the one eating the leg of the other?

**Ugly Mermaid**
In despair, some learn survival.

**Mags**
It's horrible.

**Ugly Mermaid** (*sarcatically*)
Did you expect this to be beautiful also?

**Mags**
But the sails are made of shrouds.

**Ugly Mermaid** (*shrug*)
A detail.

*Firmly.*

This is your destiny.
Hitch a ride.

**Chorus 3**
Society the wrecker
feeds us our prey.


**Scene Twenty**

*The prison.*

*The door of her cell is unlocked.* **Gaoler 1** *and* **Gaoler 2** *walk in and look at* **Mags** *who is sweating and shivering on the floor. The sea plays very quietly under this.*

**Gaoler 2**
She's still with us then?

**Gaoler 1**
She's drenched, her dress torn.

**Gaoler 2**
Sweat dissolves paper.

**Gaoler 1**
She shivers.

**Gaoler 2**
That's just the riggers.

**Gaoler 1**
The dress lies around her like shredded wings.

*Pause.*

Should I put her back on the mattress?

**Gaoler 2**
Just chuck a blanket over her.

*Into action.*

There's a girl in the next block been cutting her legs. She sharpened a toothbrush.

**Gaoler 1** (*as he puts a blanket over her*)
It's that time of night.
Four in the morning.

*Pause.*

The dead watch,
before dawn.


**Scene Twenty-One**

*The sea.*

**Mags** *is still drifting in the sea, the* **Ugly Mermaid** *swimming around her. The raft is drifting closer; we can hear it creaking, its sails flapping, the gulls and the moaning.*

**Mags**
Where is it headed?

**Ugly Mermaid** (*surprised*)
Do you care?

**Mags** (*defensive*)
Just asking.

**Ugly Mermaid**
Too late for questions.

**Mags**
All those bodies, that misery.

**Ugly Mermaid**
It's the crossing you're looking for, the next stage in despair.

*The raft creaks closer.*

**Chorus 1**
We collect fragments,
fragments of mind.
Broken like ice-floes,
that drift on the ebb.

**Chorus 2** (*shouts as if looking out to sea*)
From the starboard.

*Alarmed.*

The soul has caught a crosswind.

**Chorus 3** (*keen*)
I could stop it in its tracks.
Pin it to the mattress with the shaft of an arrow,
delivered through the air by a fletching of feathers.

*Pause.*

From a quiver to aquiver.

**Chorus 1** (*firmly*)
Our wake will toss it in.

*A splashing, paddling sound as the* **Soul** *arrives, having sailed over on a cross-current.*

**Soul** (*urgently, out of breath*)
Don't look at that raft, turn away from its sight!

**Mags**
Thought I'd lost you.

**Soul**
I caught a cross-wind.

**Ugly Mermaid**
Your soul arrives late.

**Soul**
Look away.

**Mags**
She says it's my destiny.

**Soul**
It doesn't have to be.

**Mags**
She says there's no end.

**Ugly Mermaid**
It's the ferry across.

**Soul**
She's lyin'.

**Ugly Mermaid**
Look around. See any other way out?

**Soul**
Come with me.

**Ugly Mermaid** (*scornful*)
On a mattress.

*Sarastically.*

Spoilt for choice.

**Soul**
It's the ship of fools.

**Mags**
Do I care?

**Ugly Mermaid**
It's a raft.

*Sarastically.*

There is a difference.

**Soul** (*to* **Mags**, *pleading*)
It isn't your journey.

**Mags**
How do you know?

**Soul**
Those wings on your arm are drawn to the light.


## Scene Twenty-Two

*The prison.*

*No sea sound, just the familiar footsteps and whistle of* **Gaoler 1**. *Then the Judas hole is slammed open. A beat of silence as* **Gaoler 1** *looks in.*

**Gaoler 1**
I've bought you that photo.
The photo from home.


## Scene Twenty-Three

*The sea.*

**Mags** *is drifting in the sea. The raft is much closer now as it creaks its way towards her, with the seagulls, sails flapping and corpses moaning.*

**Chorus 1**
On lookout.

**Chorus 2**
The first dogwatch.

**Chorus 3**
That beat before dawn.

**Chorus 1**
When the mind sinks
and lifelines snap.
We know we'll make a catch on this cusp of the hours
when the despair of the day meets the black of the night.

**Chorus 2**
And the mind takes no more.

**Chorus 3**
Living is not necessary but navigation is.

**Chorus 1** (*shouts towards* **Mags**, *through a loud hailer*)
Embark!

## Scene Twenty-Four

*The raft is now close to* **Mags** *and the* **Ugly Mermaid**, *the* **Soul** *and the mattress. The sails and seagulls can be heard with the gentle lapping of the waves around* **Mags**.

**Chorus 1** (*to* **Mags**)
Embark!

**Ugly Mermaid**
Get on board.

**Mags** (*giving in*)
Maybe I should.

**Soul** (*anxiously*)
You can't do this.

**Mags**
Why not?

*A boy's voice is heard calling over the sea: it is a young, distressed-sounding voice.*

**Robbie** (*voice, off*)
Mam!

**Mags** (*reacts instantly*)
Robbie!

**Robbie** (*sounding a long way away*)
    The toothpaste's all dried.

**Mags**
    My Robbie!

*At the response to* **Robbie***'s call,* **Mags** *turns in the water and as she turns she is pulled down by a violent undercurrent.*

**All Chorus**
    She turns in a tide.
    The rush of a current pulling her down.

**Mags** (*gasps*)
    I'm drowning.

*As she struggles in the water.*

    My Robbie!

*As* **Mags** *struggles in the water, going under and then resurfacing, the* **Ugly Mermaid** *and the* **Soul** *are arguing.*

**Ugly Mermaid**
    Now look what you've done.

**Soul** (*sarcastically*)
    Me?

**Ugly Mermaid**
    All those ripples you caused, stirring up water. Created an undercurrent.

**Mags** *struggles in the vicious current.*

**Mags**
    Robbie.

*She disappears under for a moment.*

**Soul**
    She's disappearing,
    under the sea.

**Ugly Mermaid**
    The end she's been looking for.

**Soul** (*anxiously*)
    I should save her.

**Ugly Mermaid**
    That's the trouble with souls, they don't understand. This is
    just how it is. Their destiny set. From the day they are born.
    Why hope for better?

**Soul** (*peering into the sea*)
    She just needed a route map.

**Mags** *bobs up again, gasping for breath.*

**Soul** (*excited*)
    I can see her hair.
    She's floating again.
    If I . . .

*Tries to reach out.*

    Reach out.

*Suddenly there is a violent, menacing, swishing sound as shoals of razor
fish come in for the kill; we hear them cutting through the water. They
slash their fins on* **Mags**' *legs, cutting her.*

**Mags** (*alarmed*)
    Something's cutting me, slashing me legs. Get off me, get
    off! They're slashing me, slashing me legs.

*In pain.*

    Get 'em off me, get 'em off!

*The fish are swishing and cutting.* **Mags** *is splashing and trying to fight
them.*

**Soul** (*alarmed*)
    And fish,
    I see fish.
    Under the water,
    quick sliver fish,
    shoals of them,
    their blades flashing.

**Ugly Mermaid**
So jump in after her.

*We hear* **Mags** *struggling in the water.*

**Soul**
I don't want to let go.

**Mags** *is struggling in the water, trying to fight the fish off.*

**Mags**
Get off me, you shite! They're cutting me, these fish are
cutting me, slashing me legs.

*The swishing is heard, the fish are after her again. The raft is close by
now; seagulls, sail flapping.*

**Chorus 1** ( *from the lookout* )
There are things,
underneath,
being stirred,
the knives of her memory,
darting from caves,
slashing the water,
sending her down.

**Mags**
I'm bleeding.

*Panicky.*

Get off me, get off me.

*She is fighting to get back to the surface. The water is chaotic as the fish
go for her and she fights them and struggles for the surface.*

**Mags**
I can't hold on.

*Calls.*

Robbie!

**Mags** *is sinking deeper and deeper into the water. All other sounds apart
from the sound of her sinking have now gone for a moment; we are drifting
deep under the sea with her. Then silence.*

## Scene Twenty-Five

*The sea.*

*The raft drifts towards the* **Soul** *Seagulls, sails, etc.*

**Chorus 1** (*on lookout, calls*)
She sinks from our course
into death's deep dark vale.

**Chorus 2**
Or Davey Jones' locker.

**Chorus 3**
Now can I shoot that damn soul?

**Chorus 1**
Behave yourself.


## Scene Twenty-Six

*Under the sea.*

**Mags** *is sinking deeper and deeper into the water. Apart from the sound of her sinking all other sounds have now gone.*


## Scene Twenty-Seven

*The prison.*

*As* **Gaoler 1** *unlocks the cell door he whistles 'Bobby Shaftoe'. The door opens, he walks in.*

**Gaoler 1** (*looking at photo*)
Here it is. Nice-looking lad. Where shall I put it?

*He walks towards her.*

Come on love, it's the photo, your boy – what's his name?

*He gets closer, sees she isn't moving or breathing.*

Jesus Christ! Now what you done?

*Pushes an alarm bell and shouts down the corridor.*

Get re-susc and fast! She's not breathing.

## Scene Twenty-Eight

*The sea.*

*The raft creaks, sails flap, seagulls call, slight moaning. The raft can be heard coming closer.*

**Chorus 1**
Strange, how one thought,
one little memory,
a ripple from the soul,
can turn things around,
stir up the waters.
Make them so frail
even despair ain't enough.
Re-chart a destiny,
re-chart it for death.

**Chorus 2**
It's that time of night.
Four in the morning.

*Pause.*

The dead watch,
before dawn.

**Chorus 3**
And that damn soul still clings,
floats,
like a turd that just won't go down.

**Chorus 1** (*firmly*)
Not for long.
We'll drift slowly,
the heaviness of our wake will toss the soul in.

## Scene Twenty-Nine

*Under the sea.*

**Mags** *is sinking deeper and deeper into the water. Apart from the sound of her sinking, the rhythmic throb of a propeller can be heard as a submarine makes its way towards her. Suddenly* **Mags** *is pulled into the submarine and the metal lid shut tight.*

*Silence.*

## Scene Thirty

*The sea.*

*The raft is heading towards the* **Soul***. Sails, gulls, moaning.*

**Chorus 3** (*on watch*)
  She's been swallowed by a whale.

**Chorus 2**
  Like Jonah.

**Chorus 3**
  Or Moby Dick.

**Chorus 2** (*arguing*)
  He wasn't swallowed.

**Chorus 1**
  I think if you look closely
  you'll see she's been swallowed,
  by a submarine.

**Chorus 3** (*a thought*)
  Does anyone know where the blue whale goes?

**Chorus 2**
  Put that crossbow away.

**Chorus 3**
  She's gone down, the soul has to follow.

**Chorus 1**
  We have to do this carefully.

**Chorus 2**
Society likes to keep its name clean.

**Chorus 1**
We'll toss her in, on the wake of our wash.


### Scene Thirty-One

*The submarine.*

*Gradually in the silence we become aware of a gentle rhythmic pumping sound like a heartbeat. It is the* **Submariner** *who is simultaneously operating the pedals of his submarine with his foot, cranking a handle with his hand and steering with the rudder under his arm.*

**Mags**
Am I dead?

*As the* **Submariner** *pumps, he speaks this to the rhythm of the pumping. He is out of breath from the effort.*

**Submariner**
It's that space just before.
The submarine in between, the rut and the rage.
The day of dead reckoning.
A short shrift of time.
An oxygen bubble
while everything slows.

**Mags**
Who are you?

**Submariner**
Bobby Shaftoe, the ancient submariner.
The ferryman,
ferrying you down,
down to the deep dark subconscious.
Crossing you over.

**Mags**
My mouth's full of salt.

**Submariner**
   The bitters of life.
   The blood, sweat and tears.
   The gall of the sea.
   The salt taste of madness and dread.

**Mags**
   What you doing?

**Submariner**
   I have to keep pumping.
   Pumping salt water into the vessel,
   to pull us down,
   down to the depths.

*Pumping, etc.*

   Negative buoyancy.

*Out of breath.*

   While we drift past your life.

*Out of breath.*

   It's hard work, this dying.

*He explains what he is doing.*

   I have to keep pumping with this foot,
   and cranking that handle,
   while steering this rudder under my arm.

**Mags**
   Where does that light come from?

**Submariner**
   Why all the questions?

**Mags**
   Just askin'.

**Submariner**
   Foxfire, a fungi, it lights up the compass,
   gives me my bearings
   to navigate your death.
   Take you down to the depths.

## Scene Thirty-Two

*The prison.*

*Sounds of prison. Alarm still ringing. Other prisoners, aware something has happened, are banging on their bars and shouting.*

**Gaoler 2**
She's choked on her vomit.

**Gaoler 1**
I can't feel a pulse.

**Gaoler 2**
Start pumping.

**Gaoler 1**
I don't like her colour, this grey.

**Gaoler 2**
I'll try giving her breath.

**Gaoler 1**
I'll try her heart.

*Pumps.*

One.
Two.

*Fade out as he pumps.*


## Scene Thirty-Three

*In the submarine.*

*The strange pumping noises continue as they sink down into the sea.*

**Submariner**
There goes the flotsam, the jetsam and lagan,
and there lies the wreck –

**Mags**
A ship?

**Submariner**
    – of your life.

**Mags**
    Like the hulk of a whale.

**Submariner**
    The bow broken.
    Arse over tit.
    A shadow from the mast,
    marking the grave.

**Mags**
    And the sails, like wings shredded in a fight.

*Sadly, as if realising something.*

    How quick was death,
    how slight the crossing.

**Submariner** (*breathlessly*)
    Not if you're the one pedalling it ain't.

**Mags**
    All my living was done to disappear.
    To sink.
    Sink beneath the surface of the roaring world.
    To let go of the deadness,
    the quickening terror, and the fear that consumed me.

*Pause.*

    But now in the darkness I see colour,
    as fish fly thoughts from the deadness of my mind.
    Each one an idea,
    a dream I had once,
    a game I played with Robbie.

*Pause.*

    In this darkness there's a light so bright you can't see it.

## Scene Thirty-Four

*The prison.*

**Gaoler 2** *is still trying mouth-to-mouth resuscitation, rhythmically counting and breathing. As she stops breathing into* **Mags'** *mouth,* **Gaoler 1** *starts pumping her heart again. Their actions mirror the actions of the* **Submariner**.

**Gaoler 1** (*counting as he pumps the heart*)
> One.
> Two.
> Three.
> Four.
> Five.

**Gaoler 2** (*breath*)
> One.

*Breath.*

> Two.

*Pause as they look at her.*

> Reckon we've lost her.

**Gaoler 1**
> I'm not giving up yet.

*Counting as he pumps the heart.*

> One.
> Two, three, four, five.

**Gaoler 2** (*breath*)
> One, two.


## Scene Thirty-Five

*The sea. The raft creaks along close to the* **Soul**.

## Chorus 1
> The soul still perches
> precariously.

A wake on the watch.
Time she fell in.

**Chorus 2**
In the wake of our trail.

**Chorus 3**
On the wake of her death.

*Holding up crossbow.*

Take aim!

**Chorus 1**
No!

**Chorus 2**
Prepare to fall in, soul.

**Soul**
Leave me alone, I don't want to drown.
Stop disturbing the water,
creating great waves.

**Chorus 3**
An arrow would be quicker.

**Chorus 2**
That would spell murder.

**Chorus 1**
Lack of care must look like an accident.
Give them enough rope,
and close the door.

**Chorus 3** (*suggestion*)
So say the arrow slipped.

**Chorus 2**
We don't want blood on our grave-clothes.
Shrouds need to stay white.

**Soul** (*pleads*)
Can't you move away a little?
Just go past slowly.
Leave me alone?

**Chorus 1**
    We can't change your destiny, that's not our course.

*A great wave from the wake of the raft passes the mattress and upturns it.
We hear a splash as the* **Soul** *falls in.*

**Chorus 3** (*through loudhailer*)
    Soul overboard!


**Scene Thirty-Six**

*The prison.*

**Gaoler 1** *is still trying to massage* **Mags'** *heart.* **Gaoler 2** *is
alternating the heart massage with mouth-to-mouth.*

**Gaoler 1** (*counting as he pumps the heart*)
    One.
    Two.
    Three.
    Four
    Five.

**Gaoler 2** (*breath*)
    One.

*Breath.*

    Two.

*Pause as* **Gaoler 2** *tries to find a pulse again.*

    Nothing.
    No pulse.
    We might as well stop.

**Gaoler 1**
    So we just give up? Accept her death? One less for the
    body-count? Her life not worth a salt.

**Gaoler 2**
    We tried.

**Gaoler 1**
By locking her up?
By giving her shrouds to stitch every day?

**Gaoler 2**
Makes a change from mailbags.

**Gaoler 1**
At least *they* carry a suggestion of hope . . . of deliverance.

*Pause.*

What must it feel like to stitch shrouds, with your destiny so uncertain any one of them could be yours? Are we Zeus to inform the fates that spin and measure and *snip* the threads of these poor young girls' lives?

*Resolute.*

We're not giving up yet.

*Starts the heart massage again.*

One, two.

**Gaoler 2**
But she's gone.

**Gaoler 1** (*continuing massage*)
Three, four, five.


**Scene Thirty-Seven**

*The sea. The raft creaking, etc.*

**Chorus 1**
With the soul gone, the sea flatlines.

*A beat of silence as they float on the calm, dead sea.*

**Chorus 2** (*calling from lookout*)
Not quite!

**Chorus 1**
What?

**Chorus 2** (*shouts, pointing*)
Over there.

**Chorus 3**
That's just the dogfish feeding on seagull.

**Chorus 2** (*pointing*)
No, further out, over there on the edge.

**Chorus 1** (*peering*)
A blip of the heart, a false dawn of hope?

**Chorus 3** (*worried*)
Or a storm.

**Chorus 1** (*panic*)
Reef the shrouds.
Batten down corpses.
Force ten heading this way.


## Scene Thirty-Eight

*In the submarine.*

*The strange pumping noises continue as they sink further down into the sea.*

**Mags** (*with an energy and determination not heard before*)
Over there! Steer me over there!

**Submariner** (*doesn't want to*)
The idea is we drift.

**Mags** (*urgently*)
I saw something, something white, floating down past my life.

*Insistent.*

Take me towards it.

**Submariner** (*not keen*)
That smacks of direction.

**Mags** (*firmly*)
I want to know what it was.

**Submariner** (*worried*)
  And enquiry.

**Mags** (*bossily*)
  Steer this thing forward, take me close to the wreck, so I can
  look in, see what it was.

**Submariner**
  It's getting a bit late for all this.

**Mags** (*insistent*)
  Crank that handle.

*Firmly.*

  Move us forward.

*We hear the handle being cranked. The submarine gets closer to the wreck.*

**Mags** (*sees what she is looking for*)
  See! Over there! Like paper, it clings, to the anchor.

**Submariner** (*explains*)
  Your soul, floated down.

**Mags**
  But I left that clinging, clinging onto a mattress,
  calling for help.

**Submariner**
  S.O.S., the seaman's curse.

**Mags**
  Why curse?

**Submariner**
  Look at the seabed – all those shells, husks of souls petrified
  by dread.

**Mags**
  But the soul is a butterfly, I read it in a book when I was a kid.

**Submariner**
  No book is gospel.

**Mags** (*firmly*)
  I know souls have wings.

**Submariner**

> Only if they're allowed to hope.
> Otherwise they sink to the bottom,
> marinated in dread,
> become shells.

**Mags** (*feeling guilty*)

> She was scared of the salt, wanted to hold on, hold on to
> hope, aim for the land, see Robbie again.

**Submariner**

> And now it's all just shipwrecks and shells.

**Mags** (*a thought*)

> If we can move forward –

**Submariner**

> Now what?

**Mags**

> Then we can move up.

**Submariner** (*not happy*)

> It's bloody hard work. I'd have to pump out all the water we
> took on to get down here.

**Mags** (*firmly*)

> So get pumping, set the compass aloft. I want to go up,
> catch my soul on the cusp of this thing. Pull her back from
> the brink, take her out of this dread.

**Submariner** *tries to pump the water out while cranking the handle
and steering the rudder.*

**Submariner**

> Resurrection is as complicated as dying.

**Mags** (*very firm*)

> I don't care! I want to do it.

**Submariner** (*fed up*)

> Now you raise hope.

*As he struggles with the pedals, etc.*

Why didn't you think of this before you stuck needles in
your arm and nooses round your neck?

**Mags**
The shingle of my life rises up to my throat, drawn by a
sense of direction, a desire for . . .

## Scene Thirty-Nine

*The prison.*

**Gaoler 2** *has just finished pumping* **Mags**' *heart. Suddenly,*
*unexpectedly,* **Mags** *is violently sick.*

**Gaoler 1** (*relieved*)
That's my girl, get it all out. The stuff of life.

## Scene Forty

*The sea.*

*With a loud splash,* **Mags** *breaks the surface of the sea. It is very*
*stormy. She is holding the* **Soul** *tightly and swimming for the mattress.*

*She is struggling with the effort of swimming against the stormy sea.*

**Mags**
Hold on, just hold on tight. We can make for the mattress.
I'll swim for us both – hold your fragile wing in my hand,
hold it tight. Salvage my soul from the savage salt of the
sea, swim against this storm. A passion rising in my mind as
I haul up from its depths, a vessel of courage that lurked in
its caverns.

*Pause.*

Past the still, stale, pulse of a life drifted.
Into the pitch and yaw of waves in a storm,
that quickens my blood,
and hawks up the gall.
When my mind fell and my heart failed you clung on,

wouldn't give up.
And now in the rage of this thought I struggle to save you,
to save my soul,
to chart back to the shore.

*Pause.*

*Music of Jeff Buckley starts to play quietly underneath as the sea sounds start to fade.*

So stay close, soul,
we'll make it back to the land,
where I'll swallow you whole.


## Scene Forty-One

*The prison.*

*No sea sounds, just the Jeff Buckley music underneath as* **Mags** *is sick again.*

**Gaoler 1**
That's my girl, get it all out.

**Gaoler 2** (*disgusted*)
Where did all this come from?

**Mags**
I'm making room for my soul.

*Fade out on Jeff Buckley, 'Hallelujah'.*